Walk Worthy

Guidelines for
the Christian life

Peter Jeffery

BRYNTIRION PRESS

© Peter Jeffery, 2000
First published 1979
Reprinted 1981
Second edition 1984
Reprinted 1986, 1988, 1994
Third edition 2000

ISBN 185049 168 2

Cover design: Mike Fryer, Applications

Published and typeset by the Bryntirion Press
Bryntirion, Bridgend CF31 4DX, Wales, UK
Printed by Creative Print and Design Limited

Contents

Preface to
Third Edition

It is over twenty years now since *Walk Worthy* was first published, and it has been reprinted several times since. This third edition is more than a reprint. It has been re-written with new material added to several chapters. Also there are six new chapters on subjects like Abortion and Drugs, which were not so much of a problem for young Christians twenty years ago.

Peter Jeffery
March 2000

Introduction

This book is written for those who have recently become Christians. That does not mean that it is written for teenagers. The new convert may be sixteen or sixty, but he or she will still face the same problems. Some of the subjects dealt with obviously have particular application to the teenager, but most of them are issues which all new Christians grapple with in the early years after conversion. Wherever possible, the book ought to be read as a sequel to *All Things New*, the intention being to cover more fully in this booklet some of the points that were made in that publication.

Like every other pastor of a church, it has been my privilege and responsibility to seek to guide young Christians through these problems. On many occasions I have wished that I had a book to give them that would be brief and yet helpful. This book is an attempt to meet that need in my own ministry. There is nothing special or unique here—indeed, it could have been written by almost any pastor. I can only trust that it will be helpful to many new Christians, that they 'might walk worthy of the Lord unto all pleasing, being fruitful in every good work, and increasing in the knowledge of God' (Colossians 1:10 AV).

Peter Jeffery
1979

1
Going On

To become a Christian is the greatest privilege any human being can have. Or, to put it another way, the greatest experience a human being can have is the knowledge of sins forgiven and peace with God. There is nothing to compare with this.

To see how highly the apostle Paul valued this experience, read Philippians 3:7-8. Now read on, from verse 9 to verse 14, and see that conversion is only the beginning. God intends us to have a growing and enriching experience of himself.

Salvation and the knowledge of sin forgiven is a tremendous gift, but it is not the only gift God has for us—see Romans 8:32. The 'all things' referred to here will only be experienced as we go on with Christ.

Going on with Christ means that

we grow spiritually	1 Peter 2:2; 2 Peter 3:18
we run the race patiently	Hebrews 12:1
we fight the battle bravely	1 Timothy 6:12

'Growing', 'running', 'fighting', is picture language which the New Testament uses to show that if we are to go on with Christ and become better and stronger Christians, then there has to be effort and discipline in our lives. We cannot grow unless we eat; we cannot run the race effectively unless we train; we cannot fight the battle with any hope of success unless we obey the commander's orders. Read again 1 Timothy 6:12, starting this time at verse 11 and reading through to verse 14.

Going on with Christ does not mean primarily that you start doing lots of things for God. There are many Christians who suffer from a disease called 'activism'. The symptom of this spiritual illness is that a person measures how spiritual he is by how busy he is for God. The more meetings he attends in the week, the more spiritual he thinks he is. Let us make it clear that a true Christian will love to go to church. The Sunday services and mid-week prayer meeting will be priorities for him. But running around all over the place, and being out every evening, is no necessary mark of going on with Christ.

Knowing and loving him
Going on with Christ is, first and foremost, to realise what God has done and is doing for you, and then to go on to experience this. You will never go on with Christ unless you get to know him more and more.

Your understanding of what God has done for you will grow deeper as you grasp more of the doctrine and teaching of the Bible, and this will only come as a result of earnest and diligent study of the Scriptures. Sitting under a good and faithful Bible ministry is also invaluable to understanding. As you seek to grapple with the Word of God, doctrines like election, justification and atonement, which may now confuse you, will gradually, by the illumination of the Holy Spirit, come to thrill your soul. If doctrines like these do not warm your heart and thrill your soul, then you have not properly understood them. The purpose of biblical doctrine is not merely to fill our heads with knowledge, but primarily to fill our hearts with love and make us worshippers. One flows out of the other. Correct understanding leads to true worship.

You will understand more of what God is doing for you as you more and more experience and feel his love in every aspect of your life. The more you know of him, the more you will love and trust him, and then the more you will see his power at work in your life.

The essential ingredients of spiritual growth are understanding, love, trust and experience.

The Christian is strong or weak depending upon how closely he has cultivated the knowledge of God. Progress in the Christian life is exactly equal to the growing knowledge we gain of the Triune God in personal experience. And such experience requires plenty of time spent at the holy task of cultivating God. God can be known satisfactorily only as we devote time to Him. *A. W. Tozer*

You need to believe now, as a young Christian, that the Lord Jesus Christ wants to make himself very real and precious to you. The following is the experience of a fifteen-year-old Christian who became one of the greatest preachers and soul-winners that England has ever known:

There is one verse of Scripture which, as a young believer, I used often to repeat, for it was very dear to me; it is this: 'Bind the sacrifice with cords even unto the horns of the altar.' I did feel then that I was wholly Christ's. In the marriage covenant of which the Lord speaks, when the Husband put the ring upon His bride's finger, He said to her, 'Thou hast become Mine'; and I remember when I felt upon my finger the ring of infinite, everlasting, covenant

11

love that Christ put there. Oh, it was a joyful day, a blessed day! Happy day, happy day, when His choice was known to me, and He fixed my choice on Him! That blessed rest of soul, which comes of a sure possession of Christ, is not to be imitated, but it is greatly to be desired. I know that some good people who I believe will be saved, nevertheless do not attain to this sweet rest. They keep on thinking that it is something that they may get when they are very old, or when they are about to die, but they look upon the full assurance of faith, and the personal grasping of Christ, and saying, 'My Beloved is mine', as something very danger-ous. I began my Christian life in this happy fashion as a boy fifteen years of age.

Why was Charles Spurgeon so mightily used by God in Christian service? It was because he knew God and loved his Saviour in a most real and intense way. There is no substitute for this in the Christian life.

These words of Spurgeon can encourage you to see that even though you may be quite a young Christian, you can have a 'full assurance of faith, and the personal grasping of Christ'. There is no growth in Christ without these.

The rest of the book seeks to deal with some of the obstacles that prevent the Christian from experiencing this fulness of salvation.

2
Justification and Sanctification

As you go on with Christ you will realise that the Lord has done far more for you in salvation than you ever imagined or hoped for. You came to Christ because of a conviction of sin and a need for forgiveness. When you repented and received Christ in faith as your Saviour, you were forgiven and reconciled to the Lord. You were made acceptable to God in the Lord Jesus Christ. You were justified by faith and now have peace with God.

This is glorious and thrilling, but there is more. Having been justified, God now begins in us the wondrous work of sanctification.

You may think that justification and sanctification are two rather heavy theological words that have very little to do with someone beginning the Christian life. If so, you could not be more wrong. You cannot be a Christian unless you have been justified, and the moment you have been justified the process of sanctification begins.

Justification
Justification is the sovereign work of God, whereby he declares the guilty sinner to be righteous and the rightful demands of the law satisfied.

Let us examine this definition:

- *sovereign work of God*—God does it all; the sinner plays no part at all (Romans 3:24; 4:4-5)
- *declares*—the judge pronouncing a legal verdict
- *guilty sinner*—guilty by nature (Ephesians 2:1-3) and guilty by action (Romans 3:10-23)
- *righteous*—right with God (Romans 5:1)
- *demands of the law*—God's law demands eternal death for the sinner (Romans 6:23)
- *satisfied*—legally and justly satisfied by the atoning death of Jesus (Romans 5:18-21; 3:26)

What does justification by faith mean? This is the doctrine which tells us that God has contrived a way whereby men and women can be saved and reconciled unto Himself. It is all of His doing. It tells us that God, on the basis of what He has done in His Son, our blessed Lord and Saviour, freely forgives, and absolves from all their sin, all who believe the gospel. But it does not stop at that; they are furthermore 'clothed with the righteousness of Jesus Christ' and declared to be just and righteous in God's sight. It is not only negative, there is this positive aspect also. We are clothed with the righteousness of Christ which is 'imputed' to us, 'put to our account', and so we stand accepted in the sight of God. As Romans 5 verse 19 puts it, we are 'constituted' righteous people in the presence of this holy and righteous God.   *D. M. Lloyd-Jones*

Justification has to do with our standing before the holy God. It does not make the sinner any different. It is crucial that you understand this. Listen again to Dr Lloyd-Jones:

It does not mean that we are made righteous, but rather that

God regards us as righteous and declares us to be righteous. This has often been a difficulty to many people. They say that because they are conscious of sin within they cannot be in a justified state; but anyone who speaks like that shows immediately that he has no understanding of this great and crucial doctrine of justification. Justification makes no actual change in us; it is a declaration by God concerning us. It is not something that results from what we do but rather something that is done for us. We have only been made righteous in the sense that God regards us as righteous, and pronounces us to be righteous.

Someone may ask, If justification does not make me any better, what is the point of it? The point is this. Immediately on being justified you are right with God! You could go to heaven there and then. You are accepted in Christ (Ephesians 1:6).

But God does not stop there. He immediately begins in you the process of change, called sanctification, that will make you a different person. Justification frees you from the *guilt* of sin and its condemnation. It is a once-for-all declaration by God. Then, the moment you are justified, the process of sanctification begins which frees from the *power* of sin.

Sanctification
The word sanctification is used in several different ways in the Bible, but in the New Testament it is used primarily to describe that process by which the Christian is purified in heart and mind.

God's will for you is sanctification	1 Thessalonians 4:3
This means holiness	1 Thessalonians 4:7
This God works in and through you	1 Thessalonians 5:23

Sanctification is that gracious and continuous operation of the Holy Spirit, by which He delivers the justified sinner from the pollution of sin, renews his whole nature in the image of God, and enables him to perform good works.

L. Berkhof

There is no such thing as instant sanctification. There is no easy formula to achieve holiness. Phrases like 'Let go and let God' may sound fine, but they are not quite what the Bible teaches.

God is the author of sanctification, not man. Nevertheless we are called upon to co-operate with God and are held responsible to strive for an ever-increasing sanctification by using the means that God has provided for us. Read 2 Corinthians 7:1; Colossians 3:5-14; 1 Peter 1:22.

No one attains to complete sanctification in this life (1 Kings 8:46; 1 John 1:8). Yet the Scripture tells us that the saints in heaven are completely free from the power of sin (Hebrews 12:23; Revelation 14:5). This means that our sanctification is completed either at death or immediately after.

So far as we are concerned now, sanctification means that the power of sin is being overcome in us. The dominion or reigning power of sin has already been broken. Read Romans 6. This great chapter reminds us that whereas we were once the slaves of sin (it dominated us, controlled us and dictated the pattern of our life), that has now changed. We are in Christ. We are dead to sin (v.11). That is, the person that I was before, I no longer am. Before, I was under sin. Now that I am a new creature in Christ Jesus, sin has no authority over me. It has no power to make me obey it.

This does not mean that sin does not bother the Christian. Of course it does, but because its absolute authority and reign have ceased, we can now triumph over it. We are no longer slaves of sin, under its heel and dominion. We are enemies of sin, fighting and resisting its evil influences. We do not obey it (v.12). We do not yield to it (v.13). We mortify (put to death) sin's advances in us (Romans 8:13; Colossians 3:5).

All this is not easy. It involves effort and determination, and it is only possible because 'we know that our old self was crucified with him [Christ] so that the body of sin might be rendered powerless, that we should no longer be slaves to sin' (Romans 6:6).

Even though we are Christians, there remains much of the old sinful nature in us. This must not be pandered to. It must be resisted and fought, and our new nature must be allowed to rule (Ephesians 4:20-32). It is as we do this that our lives are made better, holier, and more Christlike, because sanctification affects every part of us:

understanding	Jeremiah 31:33-34
will	Ezekiel 36:25-27
passions	Galatians 5:24
conscience	Hebrews 9:14

God delights to see 'good works' in his people—not as a means of salvation (Ephesians 2:8-9), but as the product of salvation that brings glory to God our Saviour (Matthew 5:16).

'Good works' are the necessary evidence of faith. This is what James pressed for in his epistle in chapter 2. Look, for example, at verse 17: 'Faith', he says 'if it hath not works, is dead, being alone.' In the next verse he says, 'I will show thee my faith by my works.' Again in verse 20 he says, 'Faith without works is dead.' 'Good works', then, are the necessary evidence that a man is a true believer. The old commentator on the Bible, Matthew Henry, wrote, 'If religion has done nothing for your tempers, it has done nothing for your souls.' In Ephesians 2, verse 10, Paul says 'For we are his workmanship, created in Christ Jesus unto good works, which God hath before ordained that we should walk in them.'

E. F. Kevan

Differences

The differences between justification and sanctification can be summed up as follows:

- Justification is all of God. Man plays no part. But whilst sanctification is also the work of God, we are expected to co-operate.
- Justification is instantaneous; it is a once-for-all thing. You are as justified now as you will ever be, and you are as justified as any other Christian. Sanctification, however, is a process. It begins at salvation and goes on for the rest of our life. The Christian can grow in sanctification, and he can also decline in it (backsliding). All Christians are at different stages of sanctification.
- Justification makes us acceptable to God. Sanctification is to make us like Jesus. Union with Christ is the foundation of sanctification. It is because we are *in* Christ that we are called to be *like* Christ.

Salvation is like being pulled out of a raging sea when waves were about to engulf you. You have been saved and placed safely upon the rocks. The waves cannot harm you there. You are safe—safe on the Rock Christ Jesus.

But salvation is more than a rescue operation. You must

18

now go on to enjoy the life you were saved for. You are on the rock, and in front of you is a seemingly unclimbable steep cliff. You realise you could no more climb that yourself than you could have got out of the water yourself. Again, I stress, you are safe on the rock, but you want to go on and upward to the fuller life. The question is, how? Then you see a rope hanging down from the top of the cliff, and you hear a voice shouting instructions to you and saying, 'You climb, and I will pull.'

That is sanctification. You are to climb over all the seemingly impossible obstacles that would try to keep you down, and at the same time God is drawing you upward and onward.

3
Obedience

Some Christians have the mistaken idea that at conversion Jesus becomes our Saviour, and that only some time later does the Christian take Jesus to be his Lord. There is no biblical foundation at all for this teaching.

> It is altogether doubtful whether any man can be saved who comes to Christ for His help but with no intention to obey Him. Christ's saviourhood is forever united to His lordship. Look at the Scriptures: 'If thou shalt confess with thy mouth the Lord Jesus, and shalt believe in thine heart that God hath raised him from the dead, thou shalt be saved . . . for the same Lord over all is rich unto all that call upon him. For whosoever shall call upon the name of the Lord shall be saved' (Romans 10:9-13). There the LORD is the object of faith for salvation. *A. W. Tozer*

The only real proof that Jesus is your Saviour is his lordship in your life. In other words, the proof of salvation is not that you went forward in a meeting, or put your hand up, or signed a decision card. The proof is that you are a new creature; old things have passed away, and all things have become new (2 Corinthians 5:17).

When Jesus saves us, he calls us to submit to him as King and Sovereign of our life. Jesus must be both Saviour and Lord. He is not one without the other. This is true because salvation is more than the forgiveness of sin. We are saved *from* sin and *into* new life in Christ. We are saved from the lordship of Satan (Ephesians 2:2; John 8:33-34,44) *into* the lordship of Christ (John 20:28; 1 Corinthians 1:9).

The response that God requires from us to the lordship of Christ is that of obedience. There can be no substitute for obedience (1 Samuel 15:22). It was Adam and Eve's disobedience to God that gave rise to the problem of sin in our nature. In Genesis 2:16-17 and 3:11 we read what God required of them. They disobeyed, and the terrible result is that 'through the disobedience of the one man the many were made sinners' (Romans 5:19). Thank God that the same verse goes on to say, 'through the obedience of the one man [Jesus Christ] the many will be made righteous.' By the grace of God you have been saved, or made righteous. So now God requires from you obedience to the authority and lordship of the Lord Jesus Christ.

Obedience is the key to everything in the Christian's life. We see early on in the Bible (Exodus 19:5) that obedience is essential to blessing. Peter opens his first letter by reminding us that we are saved to obey God (1 Peter 1:2). In verse 14 he comes back to it, and there it is again in verse 22. In John's first letter obedience is a test of salvation (1 John 2:3-4).

The secret of true obedience is a close personal relationship with the Lord. It is Christ's nearness and presence that keeps us from disobedience and sin (John 15:1-10). Obedience is not meant to be a cold, mechanical, slavish thing brought about by fear. Rather is it the response of a heart that knows and loves the Lord (Psalm 40:8; John 4:34). It is because of this that fellowship with God and obedience to God are inseparable. We are not called upon to obey harsh, unreasonable laws, but rather to obey God. 'Obey my voice', says God in Jeremiah 7:23.

21

It is interesting to note that the expression 'obey the commandments' is very seldom used in Scripture. Rather we nearly always find the words, 'obey my voice' or 'obey me'. This teaches us that obedience is a response in the Christian to God himself. If you love the Lord, you will obey him (1 John 5:3). If you delight to acknowledge Christ as your Saviour, then you must also with equal delight bow before his lordship.

A test
Have you obeyed the Lord concerning

other Christians?	Galatians 6:10
regular worship and fellowship?	Hebrews 10:25
Bible study?	2 Timothy 2:15
baptism?	Acts 2:38
your pastor(s)?	Hebrews 13:17

How is it possible that a Christian can unreservedly accept the Bible as the infallible, inspired Word of God, and yet still disobey its commandments? It is because he or she has lost the reality of the presence of the God of the Word. Correct beliefs are not enough to ensure obedience, but a right relationship to God will. Given that, you too will acknowledge that the commandments of the Lord are not grievous.

4
The Christian and the Local Church

Walking with Christ means walking and worshipping with Christ's people. This means we should think about our links with Christians in the area in which we live.

Church membership

Some Christians feel that there is no point in church membership. They argue that they have been part of the universal church of Christ since they were born again, and that the Scriptures say nothing about any other kind of church membership. What is the answer to this?

The word 'church'

The New Testament uses the word 'church' in two ways. First, there is the use as in Ephesians 5:25—'Christ loved the church, and gave himself up for her'. Here the reference is to the universal church, the whole company of the redeemed in every place, at every time. It is *the* church, the church to which all Christians belong the moment they are saved. Secondly, there is the use as in 1 Corinthians 1:2—'To the church of God in Corinth'. Here the reference is to the local church, the Christians in the city of Corinth who met together in fellowship and worship. It is not *the* church, but *a* local church.

New Testament practice

Throughout the New Testament it is assumed that every believer is a member of a local church. It is taken for granted that Christians, who from the moment they are saved have become members of the universal church, should by a conscious effort on their part become members of a local church also. In Acts 2:47 those who believed were spoken of as people whom the Lord 'added to the church' (AV). The context here makes it clear that the word 'church' refers to the local church at Jerusalem: 'And the Lord added to their number daily those who were being saved.' Unless New Testament believers were expected to be committed to a local church, the following Scriptures would be meaningless: Acts 6:3; Acts 14:23; Hebrews 10:24-25; 13:17.

Some Christians would answer: 'We accept all this; we do not believe in being spiritual butterflies flying from church to church; but we do not see the need for formal membership, with our names placed on a membership list.' And so they ask, 'What is the value of formal church membership?' Our answer is that while it is true that some evangelical churches do not have a membership list, the vast majority do, because they have found over the years that this is the best way of maintaining the *purity, order* and *discipline* of the church.

Purity

Only born-again believers should be members of the local church. The practice of having a recognised church membership represents a sincere effort to see to it that this is the case. As long as there is a list of members, no one can assume that people are members simply because they attend the services. The system may fail sometimes and unregenerate people may come into membership, but in a true gospel church that should be a very rare thing indeed. This may not be the only way of preserving the purity of the church, but it is the way that many evangelical churches have found to work satisfactorily.

Order

Scripture says that things should be done 'decently and in order' (1 Corinthians 14:40 AV), and the practice of having church membership is one way of seeking to fulfil this. Peter tells the church at Jerusalem, 'choose . . . from among you' (Acts 6:3) men suitable to be deacons. Who constitutes the 'you' in that request? Is it everyone who attends the church? Is it casual worshippers as well as the regular ones? It is easy to say that it is every regular worshipper who is born again. But who is to decide who is born again and who is not?

Church membership does not, of course, guarantee that a person is truly saved. But before people are received into membership, they would at least have to satisfy the church leaders that they have a credible testimony of salvation, and that their life bears evidence of God's regenerating grace. Thus, when the local church needs elders and deacons, it looks to the Lord to provide them through its membership. As far as is humanly possible, the acknowledgement of membership has eliminated the element of doubt and confusion as to who is a Christian, and who is therefore eligible to be considered for leadership in the church. There will be some who are undoubtedly born again, but who will refuse church membership. Such refusal is sad, because their usefulness and service in the local church will inevitably be severely restricted in consequence.

Discipline

When a Christian becomes a member of a local church, he or

she puts himself/herself under the pastoral care and discipline of that church (Hebrews 13:17). In other words, the pastor, the elders, the church and the individual Christian know exactly where they stand in relation to each other. Scriptural discipline, if it is ever necessary, is then applied in the context of a fellowship of Christians who not only love and respect one another, but who have committed themselves one to the other in church membership.

Membership is a commitment to the life and work of a local church. The *advantages* and *responsibilities* of such membership are great.

Advantages
You are entitled to the pastoral care of the church. This is no small thing (see next section). Coupled with this,

> We must never forget that when a believer is received into membership, not only does he pledge himself to the church, but the church pledges itself to him. When it accepts a new member by vote, it is not merely acknowledging that he is a Christian and entitled to membership, but also opening to him its arms of love and committing itself to serving him. 'All that believed were together, and had all things common' (Acts 2:44). Thus not only has the new member a responsibility to the church, but the church has responsibilities to him.
> *G. Eric Lane*

These two things are a great advantage to any Christian, especially to someone young in the faith.

Responsibilities
Regular attendance; using your gifts and talents; spiritual,

moral and financial support—these are some of the responsibilities that a church member must take seriously. If you are benefiting from the ministry of the church, it is your duty to help to maintain that ministry by your prayers and also by your giving. It is also the responsibility of the members to see that the pastor and his family have a reasonable standard of living. And reasonable, in this context, ought to mean no less than the average salary of his congregation.

Pastoral care

The church is not an institution devised by men; it has been founded by God himself. As we have seen, it is God's intention that we grow in the Christian faith, and one of the main functions of the church is to help this growth. To this end, we are told in Ephesians 4:11, God gives to certain men in the church the ability to teach and help. The following verse tells us what they are to do, and verses 13 and 15 show that all this is given in order to turn spiritual infants into mature believers.

The Christian's attitude towards those who are involved in positions of leadership in his church is explained very clearly in the New Testament. Read 1 Thessalonians 5:12-13; 1 Timothy 5:17; Hebrews 13:7,17. These men shoulder great responsibility and need the earnest prayers of their people.

Discipline

Part of their God-given responsibility is to administer discipline in the church, and it is your great privilege as part of the church to be under such pastoral discipline. Let me emphasise, this is a privilege. To have older, mature Christians who care enough about your spiritual growth to rebuke you when you are wrong is nothing but a privilege.

Today, discipline has become almost a dirty word in many

sections of society. Everyone wants to do just as they please. That is the attitude of the world. You, however, are no longer 'of the world' (John 17:14). You are a Christian, and what you do and say affects other Christians and, more importantly, brings either glory or shame on God's name. If you do wrong, it is necessary for your own well-being (Galatians 6:1), for the peace of the church (Romans 16:17), and for the honour of God, that you be told.

Will you be willing to accept this discipline if and when it is necessary?

Keep your heart open to the correction of the Lord and be ready to receive His chastisement regardless of who holds the whip. The great saints all learned to take a licking gracefully—and that may be one reason why they were great saints.   *A. W. Tozer*

As the shepherd sees the dangerous precipice or the lurking wolf before the sheep do, so an experienced minister can frequently see a Christian heading for danger. At such a time a faithful pastor will go to his member before his member comes to him and warn him of his danger, and for this he will (or should) be very thankful. Of course the grass grows greener by the cliff edge and he may initially resent being hauled away from it, but he will eventually see the wisdom of the shepherd's action. The knowledge of this should give a great sense of security to one who becomes a church member. He will feel he is not having to face the world and the devil alone. He knows he cannot trust himself and that he is inexperienced, and is greatly strengthened by the knowledge that one more mature and gifted is there to lead him along and protect him, and to be on hand when need arises.

G. Eric Lane

In Psalm 23 David says that the Lord, his shepherd, restores his soul when he wanders away. The Lord accomplishes this restoration in various ways, but one of them is through the pastor, elders and deacons of the church, the under-shepherds of the flock. These men have been charged by God to 'watch for your souls' (Hebrews 13:17 AV).

> Your spiritual improvement, your everlasting salvation, is his object; and therefore he must not, to spare your feelings, endanger your souls. It were cruel kindness in the physician, to save a little present pain, to allow a fatal disease to fix its roots in the constitution, which must by and by produce far more suffering than what is now avoided, and not only suffering, but death. *John Brown*

Leading the people of God is no easy task. Look at the trouble Moses had (Numbers 21:5), and Paul too (2 Corinthians 13:1-3). A pastor's responsibilities are enormous and the demands on his time exhausting, but if he is a true man of God you will have cause to thank God for him. He is not infallible and he will make mistakes, but he is God's servant.

Read again 1 Thessalonians 5:12-13; 1 Timothy 5:17; Hebrews 13:7,17. Do these verses describe your attitude?

Fellowship

The moment you become a Christian you become part of the great family of God; you are a fellow citizen with the people of God and belong to the household of God (Ephesians 2:19). When God saved you he did not mean you to live in isolation.

You are meant to be part of the church and to enjoy fellowship with other believers. One of the most beautiful things you discover after conversion is the blessed bond you have with other Christians.

> Fellowship . . . means 'sharing together' or a 'having in common'. It implies first of all that there is something which may be shared. This, of course, is the blessing of the gospel. Better still, we may say there is some One who is to be shared. This is the Lord Jesus Himself. But the word also implies that there are those among whom the sharing is experienced. You can see, therefore, that the Christian looks not only upward to the Saviour, but he looks out, right and left, toward his fellow-believers in Christ. He realises that he is not a solitary person—a kind of 'Robinson Crusoe'—but is saved in the company of others.
>
> *E. F. Kevan*

God's people are drawn from all types of background, rich and poor, black and white, clever and dull; yet they are all one in Christ. All barriers fall before the redeeming love of Jesus (Ephesians 2:14-16; Galatians 3:26-28). The New Testament abounds with examples of this.

Among the twelve apostles was Simon the Zealot, the ardent Jewish nationalist, and also Matthew the tax collector, the servant of the hated Romans. These two men would normally have hated each other, but in Christ they are one.

Sharing together
Fellowship is not a matter of a few Christians talking together about the weather or their holidays, or engaging in social chit-chat. This, of course, can be quite enjoyable, and there is no

harm in Christians having some fun together. But the uniqueness of Christian fellowship consists in being able to talk about and share together the joys, blessings and problems of our faith.

In the New Testament, fellowship manifested itself, and was encouraged, in various ways:

- In the believers' evident desire to be in the company of other believers (Acts 2:44,46; 4:23; 20:7).
- In their desire to learn of Christ and his truth, and to share their common experience of him (Acts 2:42; 20:7,11).
- In their corporate prayer life (Acts 2:42; 4:24,31; 12:5).
- In their united witnessing (Acts 4:31,33).
- In their concern for each other's welfare (Acts 2:44-45; 4:34-35; 11:27-30; Romans 12:13; 1 Corinthians 16:1-3; 2 Corinthians 8:1-4; Galatians 2:10).
- In their sharing of one another's burdens (1 Corinthians 12:26; Galatians 6:2).
- In their strengthening of one another in Christian things (Romans 15:1-3; Galatians 6:1; Hebrews 10:24).
- In missionary support (Philippians 4:14-16).
- In their gathering together at the 'communion' service (Acts 2:42; 1 Corinthians 10:16-17).

Loving each other
Sadly, there are times when fellowship is marred by quarrels and disputes. This happened even in New Testament times (Acts 6:1; 15:36-41). We must be continually on our guard, so that we shall in no way be the cause of disrupting fellowship.

The way to do this is to seek at all times to walk in the path of love, as described in 1 Corinthians 13. 'Love is patient, love is kind. It does not envy, it does not boast, it is not proud. It is not rude, it is not self-seeking, it is not easily angered, it keeps no record of wrongs.'

Remember, you can *give* offence unintentionally, but you can never *take* offence unintentionally. So do not be touchy. Love one another.

The fellowship of the church depends upon this. Our churches cannot be any more spiritual than we are as individuals. We forget sometimes that the church consists of sinners. It is true that they are sinners saved by grace, but none the less they are far from perfect. A major cause of problems in the church is that we forget this and we set too low a standard for ourselves and too high a standard for others. We expect them to behave in a way that we ourselves do not. For example, if people do not speak to us or visit us when we are ill we get upset; but do we visit others? None of us is perfect in attitude or behaviour, so let us all exercise a little tolerance. This is not to excuse sin, but a greater tolerance of each other will help us to be more loving and less critical.

There are some Christians who are very easy to get on with. Others are more difficult, but we are still all members of the household of God. So work at it. Be patient. Remember that some Christians probably find it difficult to get on with you, so be tolerant.

Fellowship is like the spokes of a wheel. The closer the spokes are to the hub, the closer they are to each other. The further away they are from the hub, the further they are from each other. In the same way, the closer you are to the Lord, the closer you will be to other believers. The more you enjoy fellowship with Christ, the more you will enjoy the fellowship of his people.

5
Worship

Probably the greatest privilege that salvation confers upon us this side of heaven is to be allowed to worship God. When we reach heaven, to worship him will be the supreme delight of the saints for all eternity. Read Revelation, chapters 5 and 7.

Man was created to be a worshipper of Almighty God, but sin ruined that. In Genesis 3 we read that when sin entered human nature it destroyed man's peace with God. Man sought to hide from God (v.8), and he has continued to do so ever since. Sin destroyed man's access to God (v.22), but in salvation these lost privileges are restored to the believer (Romans 5:1-2).

Whilst it is still true that there is something in man's nature that makes him a compulsive worshipper, the object of his worship has ceased to be Almighty God and is now some life-less god of his own making (Psalm 115:4-8). In modern terms, man worships his sport, car, garden, etc. These things dominate his life; they have become his gods.

You were like that once, but now you have a Saviour to bring you to God (John 14:6); you have a mediator (1 Timothy 2:5); an atonement has been made for your sin (Hebrews 9:11-14). This means that you can now worship Almighty God.

> Worship is to feel in the heart a humbling but delightful sense of admiring awe and astonished wonder, and to express it in some appropriate manner. Worship is awesome wonder and overpowering love in the presence of God.
>
> *A. W. Tozer*

Learn to worship

If worship is such a great privilege, it stands to reason that one of the first things you need to do after conversion is to learn to worship God.

> We're here to be worshippers first and workers only second. We take a convert and immediately make a worker out of him . . . God never meant it to be so. God meant that a convert should learn to be a worshipper, and after that he can learn to be a worker. *A. W. Tozer*

A certain degree of worship will come automatically. You will praise and worship God for what he has done for you. But worship is more than that. Read Tozer's definition again— 'admiring awe and astonished wonder'. In other words, when we realise how great and holy our God is, there comes over us a tremendous sense of awe and wonder. We then worship God not merely for what he has done for us, but for who he is and what he is. The more you know of God, the more you will worship God. The more you know God, the more you will love God, and love is the true basis of worship: 'Thou shalt love the Lord thy God with all thy heart, and with all thy soul, and with all thy might' (Deuteronomy 6:5 AV).

> It is quite impossible to worship God without loving Him. Scripture and reason agree to declare this. And God is never satisfied with anything less than all: 'all thy heart . . . all thy soul . . . all thy might'. This may not at first be possible, but deeper experience with God will prepare us for it, and the inward operations of the Holy Spirit will enable us after a while to offer Him such a poured-out fulness of love. *A. W. Tozer*

You learn to worship as you learn to appreciate the great-ness of God.

It is obvious that for any worship to be acceptable and right there must be a knowledge of God and of the nature of His holy requirements. The first and fundamental thing is to have a right idea about God . . . It is valuable to observe here that because the true worship of God depends upon His revelation of Himself, the reading and preaching of the Bible occupies such an important place in public worship.

It is impossible to have an idea of God that is too high. It is possible, however, to have an idea that is too theoreti-cal. God is to be known in the way in which He has revealed Himself. He has shown His character, His strength, and His wisdom, in the experiences of those to whom He has made Himself known. We ought to note par-ticularly two outstanding things which the Bible makes plain to us about God, namely, that God is the Creator and God is great. *E. F. Kevan*

Whether you are worshipping on your own or with other Christians in church, it is essential that you know the presence of God and delight in the wonder of his love. Forms of wor-ship may vary, but these things are of secondary importance. Whether, for example, you stand or kneel, use a prayer book or not, sing three hymns or four, are not as important as hav-ing at that time a right appreciation of God.

To worship God aright we must grasp hold of these two things: God is our Maker and God is our Lord. Any wor-ship which does not proceed on these lines must be false worship. Look up two passages which relate these truths

about God to our ways of worshipping Him: Psalm 100 and
John 3:22-24.   *E. F. Kevan*

Jesus said that those who worship God must worship him
'in spirit and in truth' (John 4:24).

To 'worship in spirit', is to worship spiritually; to 'worship
in truth', is to worship truly. They are not two different
kinds of worship; they are two different aspects of the same
worship: to worship spiritually, is in opposition to the per-
formance of mere external rites, to give to God the homage
of an enlightened mind, and an affectionate heart; to know,
admire, esteem, love, trust, and submit to Him; and to worship Him truly, is either to worship Him according to the
truth—that is, in a manner suited to the revelation He has
made of His character; or really, not merely in appearance,
but in substance—not in pretence only, but in sincerity.
Such—such alone—are the acceptable worshippers.
                                                      John Brown

It is clear that worship is much more than a pleasant emotional feeling; it must involve the mind. Our understanding of
God is crucial to true worship. But if the mind is filled with all
the right doctrines and the heart is devoid of any sense of
God's presence, there can be no true worship. Heart and mind
blend together in worship to praise and enjoy God.

Public worship
When you join other Christians for worship, do not do so
flippantly or lightheartedly. Go with reverence. It is Almighty
God whom you intend to meet. Go also with expectancy.
Expect to meet with God, and be satisfied with nothing less.

Enter into the worship with enthusiasm as well as reverence. Let the hymns be an expression of your own feelings. Sing not merely to enjoy yourself, but as part of your worship of God.

> Above all, sing spiritually. Have an eye to God in every word you sing. Aim at pleasing Him more than yourself or any other creature. In order to do this, attend strictly to the sense of what you sing, and see that your heart is not carried away with the sound, but offered to God continually.
>
> *John Wesley*

During prayer follow the thoughts and expressions and, whenever possible, identify yourself with them. Make sure that you take a Bible with you to follow the reading and preaching. Follow the preaching with serious thought and attention. If you do not understand, ask someone at the end of the service.

It is sometimes objected that in most churches the congregation does not fully enter into worship, and that what we need is more participation by the whole church. To say this is to fail to understand that in singing, praying, preaching and hearing, every person present should be actively engaged. We have already seen what John Wesley says about singing, but the same is true about the prayer and the sermon. One person will lead in prayer, but all should be praying; and you will already have discovered that there is no greater stimulant to worship than biblical preaching in the power of the Spirit. The preacher says something that causes your heart to praise and adore your Saviour. He is preaching; you are listening; but you are both worshipping.

Worship, of course, is not confined to a building or to a Sunday. It is the continual privilege of the people of God. This is your privilege now. Worship Almighty God, then, conscious of his greatness and your sinfulness. Let your heart be humbled before him, but at the same time let it overflow with praise.

Great is the mystery of godliness,
Great is the work of God's own holiness;
It moves my soul, and causes me to long
For greater joys than to the earth belong:

O let the praises of my heart be Thine,
For Christ has died that I may call Him mine,
That I may sing with those who dwell above,
Adoring, praising Jesus, King of love.

W. Vernon Higham

6
Witnessing

The last recorded words of the risen Christ to his apostles before his ascension were, 'you will be my witnesses . . .' Every Christian is called to be a witness.

Witnessing begins with caring

It begins, firstly, with caring about *the glory of God*. God is not glorified and honoured in this world because the vast majority of people do not know and love him. His truth is trampled in the mud and his name taken in vain. The only way for this to change is for people to become Christians. Look at how different your attitude to God is now, compared to what it was before you were converted. If you care enough about God's glory, you will tell people the good news of the gospel.

Witnessing begins, secondly, with caring about *people*—caring about unbelievers in their bondage and spiritual blindness. Without Christ, men and women are going to hell. Do you care? Then witness to them of the only way of salvation.

Many Christians are timid about witnessing. To counteract this a great many different methods and schemes of personal evangelism have been devised. This is all done with the best of intentions, but it does not provide the answer to the problem. It makes witnessing too mechanical and artificial, so that instead of being a natural overflow, it becomes rather like scraping the bottom of the barrel.

Witnessing flows out of worship

If witnessing begins with caring, it is also true to say that witnessing flows out of worship. Too many older Christians tell new converts that the first thing they need to do is to learn how to witness. This is wrong. The prime need of the new convert is to learn to worship. Witnessing will always be difficult unless the heart of the believer is absorbed in God.

> My heart is full of Christ, and longs
>   Its glorious matter to declare!
> Of Him I make my loftier songs,
>   I cannot from His praise forbear;
> My ready tongue makes haste to sing
> The glories of my heavenly King.

Charles Wesley is perfectly correct. Fill your heart with worship of Christ, and witness will inevitably be the overflow of your experience of God. Read Acts 2:41-47.

God may never call you to be a preacher or a missionary, but if you are a Christian he has already called you to be a witness for him in this world. In Acts 11, where we read that the gospel started spreading into all the world, God did not only use great preachers. Ordinary timid believers were used: 'Some of them, men from Cyprus and Cyrene, went to Antioch and began to speak to Greeks also, telling them the good news about the Lord Jesus. The Lord's hand was with them, and a great number of people believed and turned to the Lord' (vv.20-21). Take heart from this, and follow the example of those nameless saints.

In word and deed

You must never forget that once you are known as a Christian, everything you do is a witness. It may be a good witness or a bad witness. Your behaviour is every bit as important as your words. People will quite rightly dismiss all you say if they do not see the gospel having an effect upon your life. Witnessing, therefore, is not an occasional happening, but a twenty-four-hour business.

Your life will show where you stand with God, but it is your words, more than anything else, that will show unbelievers where they stand. The gospel *must* be spoken (Romans 10:14). The people in your home, school, factory or office need to hear of God's love and offer of salvation. If *you* do not tell them, it may well be that no one else will.

You must never confine your witnessing merely to giving a testimony of your own experience of God. This can, of course, be included, but your purpose must be to present people with the gospel. They must be shown that they are sinners (Romans 3:23), under the wrath and judgement of God (Romans 1:18) and already condemned by God (John 3:18). You must tell them that God demands repentance (Acts 3:19; 17:30) so that they can then turn in faith to Christ for salvation (Ephesians 2:4-9; John 1:12).

In your witness, do not be arrogant or aggressive. On the other hand, do not be timid or apologetic. Speak naturally and warmly of the things of God. Do not be over-concerned about proving a point and winning an argument. Be patient and loving. Do not be surprised if you are ridiculed for your strange beliefs (Acts 26:24; 1 Corinthians 4:10). Keep pointing people to Jesus. Let his name be the word most frequently upon your lips, that people may see you are Christ's servants. Be concerned for individuals.

If you had one hundred empty bottles before you, and

threw a pail of water over them, some would get a little in them, but most would fall outside. If you wish to fill the bottles, the best way is to take each bottle separately and put a vessel full of water to the bottle's mouth. That is successful personal work.   *C. H. Spurgeon*

7
Prayer

Prayer is an offering up of our desires unto God, for things
agreeable to His will, in the name of Christ, with confes-
sion of our sins, and thankful acknowledgement of His
mercies.   *Shorter Catechism*

As you read the Bible, you soon discover that one of the
factors that distinguishes the lives of all the great people
of God is prayer. Consider the following examples:

Moses	Exodus 33:12-13	David	2 Samuel 7:18-29
Daniel	Daniel 9:3-19	Paul	Ephesians 1:15-23

These were men of different temperaments and backgrounds,
but they all knew the indispensable value of prayer.

In case we are tempted to excuse ourselves by pleading that
these were great men of God, whereas we are only ordinary
Christians, James in his epistle reminds us that Elijah was 'a
man subject to like passions as we are' (5:17 AV)—or, as the
NIV translates it, 'Elijah was a man just like us.' He had the
same emotions, the same fears, the same doubts, as the rest of
us. Do you find this difficult to believe? Read 1 Kings, chapters 17, 18 and 19.

Do you sometimes feel like packing it all in and running
away? Elijah did (1 Kings 19:3). Do you sometimes feel
rather sorry for yourself and think you are all alone and no one

else cares? Elijah did (1 Kings 19:14). Yet this man was a mighty man of prayer. And so too can you be. 'The prayer of a righteous man is powerful and effective' (James 5:16).

What part does prayer play in your life? Is it something you engage in occasionally when you feel like it? Is it something you only resort to in times of trouble? Is it a daily pleasure or a daily drudgery? What part *should* prayer play in the life of a Christian?

Having seen the example of some great men, we can go further and see the example of our Saviour. Jesus started the day with prayer (Mark 1:35). He prayed always, in all circumstances, whether it was

the blessing of baptism	Luke 3:21
the joy of transfiguration	Luke 9:29
the agony of Gethsemane	Matthew 26:36-44
the temptation of flattery and applause	John 6:15; Matthew 14:23
the responsibility of great decision	Luke 6:12-13

If prayer was so important for the holy, sinless Son of God, how much more important is it for us to persevere in prayer!

Paul tells us that we are to 'pray in the Spirit on all occasions with all kinds of prayers and requests' (Ephesians 6:18). There are basically three different types of prayer, and we are to be familiar with each.

Private prayer
Jesus speaks of this in Matthew 6:6. 'Thy closet' (AV) means 'your own room' (NIV): in other words, you get away from people to be alone with God. This sort of prayer is vital; it is

not something optional, but something that *must* be included as part of our lives. Because it is so vital, it is not surprising that the devil makes it exceptionally difficult.

Experiencing difficulty in prayer is common to all Christians. You find it difficult to concentrate; you find your mind wandering; you even find yourself thinking evil thoughts. You may read of Christians spending four or five hours in prayer, and the devil tells you to compare that to your five or ten minutes in prayer—and that makes you despair of prayer altogether. But you must not do so. Do not let the devil deceive you. You are a young Christian now, but in twenty years' time you will still be having the same problems. It has nothing to do with age, and little to do with experience. It is part and parcel of the constant battle we have with the flesh and the devil.

So often our whole concept of prayer is unbiblical. We think that if prayer is difficult, it must be useless or wrong. But the words that Paul uses to describe prayer are 'wrestling' (Colossians 4:12) and 'striving' (Romans 15:30 AV). He realised that there was a great battle going on. And the Christian is never so much in the front line of the battle as when he is praying.

Our terminology is also wrong. It is popular today for Christians to describe their times of private prayer as their 'Quiet Time'. The very title gives the wrong impression. When I think of a 'quiet time', I picture a scene of tranquil contentment, feet up, dozing off, all peaceful, no problems. Praise God, there are times when prayer is easy, when our spirits are lifted up to rejoice in God; but it is not always like that. The phrase 'Quiet Time' has conditioned many Christians to think it is wrong to labour, strive and wrestle in prayer. Consequently they give up too easily—and the devil is delighted.

Often these difficulties arise before we even get to our

knees. We find it difficult to find a suitable time to pray, and it is easy then to fall into the trap of fitting it in when it is convenient. If you do that, do not be surprised to find that it is not being 'fitted in' very much at all. The devil will see to that.

I am not trying to depress you by mentioning all these problems. If you really are a Christian you will have discovered most of them already. The question is, How do we deal with them? I can give you the customary answers: fix a regular time for prayer and stick to it; if your thoughts begin to wander, pray audibly instead of silently; do not give in, but keep on striving. All these answers are important and useful, but the real answer is found in a phrase from the verse we have already quoted—'pray in the Spirit' (Ephesians 6:18).

To pray in the Spirit means that the prayer is not a mere mouthing of words, empty, dry and formal. It is quite the opposite. There is warmth, reality, passion and power. This is because the Holy Spirit creates the prayer in our heart and mind. You are not then praying out of a sense of duty or even desire, but the petitions are given by the Spirit. Not only does the Holy Spirit give the content of the prayer, but he also gives the power and ability to pray it.

How does one pray in the Spirit? You start by viewing prayer not merely as a daily devotional exercise, but as an act of private worship. You are going to meet with God, and therefore you prepare yourself. This involves discipline. You must give time to prayer. By this I mean that you must not rush into prayer, make a few requests, and then rush off again. 'Be still, and know that I am God.' You come to prayer, aware of your own sinfulness and unworthiness; then you meditate on the love and mercy of God. You shut the world out and seek to get alone with God. This is not easy. All too often we are satisfied by merely going through the motions of prayer.

You have to be spiritually minded, wanting to meet with God more than anything else. You must look to the Holy Spirit to lead and direct your thoughts.

Consider carefully the following two quotations from Dr D. M. Lloyd-Jones:

> If your heart is not warmed by thinking of the Lord Jesus when you pray you are not praying in the Spirit. The Spirit always brings us to that, always brings us to that realisation that we enter into the Holiest only 'by the blood of Jesus'. And the moment you realise that, your heart is melted and is warmed, something happens to you. That is 'praying in the Spirit'. You see, the formality is finished with and now you are in this spiritual condition. You have to realise your right to approach God, and you are enabled to do so with a 'holy boldness'.

> Is there anything on earth which is more wonderful than freedom in prayer? Do you delight in it, do you rejoice in it? When you are suddenly given freedom—you may have been struggling in prayer, finding it difficult to concentrate, finding it difficult to gather your thoughts as it were to make contact—suddenly there is a freedom given you. Have you not noticed it also in public prayer? You have been stumbling, you have been halting, you have been praying as you should with your mind, you have been ordering your thoughts, you have been gathering your petitions. It is all right, we must do that. But that is only the framework, that is the scaffolding, and you do not stop with that. Suddenly the Spirit comes and you are taken out of yourself, and the words pour out of you and you know that you are speaking to Him, and there is an exchange taking

place. You are in the realm of the Spirit and enjoying something of the glorious liberty of the children of God.

Read the last quotation again. This is what we all want to experience in prayer more and more, but it does not mean that nothing else is real prayer. It does not mean that if you are not praying in the Spirit, you are not really praying. God honours our intentions. God knows and loves us. He honours our poor, unworthy, stammering, small-faith prayer. God sees us with all our weaknesses, fears, doubts and prejudices. He is a merciful God who always hears the cries of his people. So keep on praying through all the barriers raised by the devil. Labour and strive, but above all cry to God for the Holy Spirit's aid, that you may pray in the Spirit.

Prayer meetings
Private prayer is vital, but so too is the prayer meeting, when the whole church comes together to pray. There is a lovely example of this in Acts 4:23-31.

At the beginning of your Christian life get your priorities sorted out and place your church prayer meeting at the top of your list. It is more important than the young people's fellowship, young wives' group, sisterhood meeting, or even Sunday school. If you are too busy to attend the prayer meeting, then *you are too busy.*

> No person can be a child of God without living in secret [private] prayer; and no community of Christians can be in a lively condition without unity in prayer.
>
> *Robert Murray M'Cheyne*

The devil hates prayer meetings, and is always seeking to destroy them; and so often we play into his evil hands. Some Christians pray far too long, and the majority do not pray at all. This gives rise to murmurings and criticising and staying away. It is easy to criticise a prayer meeting, but before you do so, first ask yourself if you contributed anything to help the meeting.

The prayer meeting used to be called the powerhouse of the church. That is perfectly correct. So do not despair if it takes some time to get the fire going in the boiler. Persevere. Go along not to criticise but to pray. *You* pray. You may be young in the faith, but you have as much right to pray as the oldest saint. Help to make the meeting a source of blessing to the whole church.

Praying always
There is also another aspect of prayer which is not easy to define. All one can call it is the continual spirit of prayer. You can pray without bending your knees and without closing your eyes. You can pray while you are driving the car, washing the dishes, digging the garden. In all sorts of situations you can lift up your heart to God. This is part of 'all kinds of prayer'. In the daily routine of work a problem arises, and you imme- diately commit it to God. You do not make a Pharisaic display, but silently and in a second you ask the Lord's help. Read how Nehemiah did this (chapter 2:1-5). Note the words at the end of verse 4 and the beginning of verse 5: 'Then I prayed to the God of heaven, and I answered the king'. All this happened in a split second. By some Christians this kind of prayer is called 'sending telegrams to God'. The expression is rather quaint, but you will know what it means: a simple prayer is offered like 'God, help me' or 'Thank you, Lord.'

All three kinds of prayer are important, and we are to practise them all continually.

This chapter on prayer is one of the longest in the book.

49

That is because it is of supreme importance. If a Christian's prayer life is weak, the whole of his or her life is weak. Be a person of prayer, and most other things will follow.

One last thought. You can read every book ever published on the subject of prayer, but *the only way to be strong in prayer is to pray.*

8
The Bible:
Which Version?

If you had become a Christian fifty years ago, you would in all probability have been using the Authorised Version of the Bible (AV). (That may still be the case today, of course.) At that time, although there were other versions of the Bible available, the AV had no serious rival among evangelical Christians. By today, however, the situation has changed dramatically, and the newly converted person is faced with a multiplicity of versions, which inevitably gives rise to confusion. In recent years there have been a number of major translations of the Scriptures into English. These include the RSV (Revised Standard Version, 1952), the NASB (New American Standard Bible, 1963), the NIV (New International Version, 1978), the NKJV (New King James Version, 1982), as well as one or two other translations of the New Testament.

In any congregation you will probably find four or five different versions being used, and this is liable to cause confusion, particularly for the young convert. Several years ago I was preaching on the text in Matthew 17:21—'Howbeit this kind goeth not out but by prayer and fasting' (AV). In the congregation was a young man who had only been converted a few weeks, and I could see when I gave out the text that he looked very puzzled. I discovered afterwards what his problem was: he was using an RSV Bible, and in that version

Matthew 17:21 is omitted. So my text was not in his Bible!

Translation or paraphrase?

Another more serious source of confusion is the use of a paraphrase version. A paraphrase attempts to 'take the original thought and convert it into the language of today' (K. M. Taylor)—or, to quote *The Concise Oxford Dictionary*, a paraphrase is a 'free rendering or amplification of a passage'. On the surface this sounds very helpful, but it does give rise to serious problems of accuracy.

For example, the AV, RSV and NIV are translations; but the *Living Bible*, of which many million copies have been sold since 1971, is a paraphrase. What is the difference between a translation and a paraphrase? Well, the man who is translating looks at the original Hebrew and Greek and asks the question, What does it *say*? But the man who is producing a paraphrase looks at the original languages and asks the question, What does it *mean*? You may think there is not much difference between these two questions, but there is, and they can produce different answers. The danger of a paraphrase is that it does not always translate the original accurately. Inevitably, 'What does it mean?' becomes 'What do I think it means?'— and so words and thoughts are added that are not in the original. The *Living Bible* is guilty of this on many occasions.

A glaring example of this is John 1:17. The AV reads, 'For the law was given by Moses, but grace and truth came by Jesus Christ.' The *Living Bible* reads, 'Moses gave us only the Law with its rigid demands and merciless justice, while Jesus Christ brought us loving forgiveness as well.' In this version much is added which is not biblically true. Moses did not give us *only* the law, for Jesus said, 'he wrote about me'. The law in the Old Testament was certainly not merciless, but speaks

52

of the mercy of God in many places. You will notice also that the *Living Bible* leaves out the reference to Jesus bringing *truth*.

Paraphrases may be easier to read and understand, but this in no way makes up for the inaccuracies. Such versions can be helpful, but they should only be used alongside a good translation.

What is a good translation?
Basically what the Christian requires is a translation that is accurate and understandable. Many young Christians find the AV difficult to understand: apart from the use of 'thee' and 'thou', many words have changed their meaning since the seventeenth century. So which version do you use? It is not difficult to determine what you can understand and what you cannot, but no young convert is in a position to decide which version is accurate and which is not. Here you need guidance and advice, and you would be well advised to speak to your pastor about this matter.

A clue to the issue of accuracy may be given in the attitude of the translators themselves to Scripture. Do they believe in the authority and inspiration of the Word of God? Do they agree with the teaching and doctrines of the Bible?

This is no small point. For example, the translators of many modern versions do not believe in the wrath of God. The Bible is very clear on this doctrine, but these translators reject it. Consequently, when they have to deal with a word like 'propitiation' (Romans 3:25 AV), which means Christ turning away the wrath of God from the sinner by his substitutionary death on the cross, they change the word to 'expiation' (RSV and New English Bible), which means Christ taking away our sins. It is true that Christ is an expiation for us; he did take away our sin; but that is not what Paul is saying in Romans 3:25. Here is a case where the translation of the word is affected by the doctrinal beliefs of the translators. As Dr Lloyd-Jones puts it, 'It is an example of a translation that has already become exposition. It has put a word which has a different meaning in place of the word used by the Apostle.'

Of the many modern versions, some at least have been translated by men who are faithful to the authority and meaning of Scripture, such as the NASB, NKJV and NIV. The NIV was described in *Evangelical Times* as 'The best version in the English language. Eminently suitable for private and public use, as well as for memory work.'

It must be said that many recently converted Christians have no trouble with the AV. But if you do find it difficult and you want a modern version, try the NIV or the NKJV.

9
Valuing the Bible

Believing the Bible has traditionally meant, for evangelical Christians, accepting it as the inspired, inerrant Word of God. This is far more than believing that the Bible *contains* the Word of God. For the evangelical the Bible *is* God's Word. Because of its unique qualities it is the supreme authority for what we believe and the way we live our lives.

Much has been written on what the words 'inspired' and 'inerrant' mean, and I do not wish to add to that in this chapter other than briefly to define their meaning. 'Inspiration' means that those who actually wrote the sixty-six books of the Bible did not give their own opinion but were guided and directed by the Holy Spirit—'men spoke from God as they were carried along by the Holy Spirit' (2 Peter 1:21). In the words of E. J. Young, 'inerrant' means that 'the Scriptures possess the quality of freedom from error. They are exempt from the liability of mistake, incapable of error. In all their teachings they are in perfect accord with the truth.'

If the Bible is inspired and inerrant, it must inevitably be the Christian's supreme authority for what he believes and how he lives. The believer's great concern must be to please God, and to live for the glory of God. The Bible tells us how to do this, because in his book God declares his will for our lives. If we really accept the authority of the Bible, we will test everything by what the Scriptures say. This is why it is so important for Christians both to know and believe their Bible.

If the Bible is not our authority, then something else will be, and in all probability it will be our own human understanding. The choice, then, is between what I think and what God has said. To make our own opinion our authority is really a most flimsy foundation on which to build.

In recent years there have been two major shifts in the thinking of evangelicals towards the Bible. Some no longer wholeheartedly accept the inspiration of Scripture, and that undermines any claim that the Bible exercises real authority in their lives. Others, whilst still accepting an orthodox doctrine of Scripture, in actual fact deny by their lives what they say they believe. These two attitudes have been around for a long time (see 2 Timothy 4:3-4; Titus 1:15-16), but in recent years they have been more pronounced.

No authority

If there is no supreme authority, then there can be no absolute standards and everything becomes relative. Nothing is right, nothing is wrong. It just depends upon how each individual sees things. So in the world there are no longer any moral standards, and in the church there are no longer any absolute truths. For instance, it is clear from the New Testament that the church in the first century believed in the reality of hell, but today if you believe this you are considered to be very strange, rather outdated and certainly lacking in love.

There is a very clear link between the morals of the world and the lack of doctrinal certainty of the church. When the church has to debate whether or not it should conduct marriage services for homosexuals, it is not only rejecting the biblical teaching but is also encouraging sin. Very often the reason given for such discussion is that we should love and not condemn. This sounds very laudable, but basically it is a flawed argument. For instance, no one loved like Jesus, but some of his condemnations in Scripture are scathing. He called the religious leaders of his day a brood of vipers (Matthew 23:33), and he said that some of them belonged to the devil (John 8:44).

Because the Bible is so often rejected today we have a very confused understanding of what love is. It is not loving to mislead people by saying that everyone is going to heaven if God in his Word very clearly says this is not so. The same is true in the moral realm. A young woman falls in love with a man. They begin seeing each other, and before long they are sleeping together. She speaks passionately of how much she loves him, but when confronted with the fact that he is married and has three children, all she can say is, 'I know, but I cannot help it. I love him.' What has this so-called love to do with the love spoken of in 1 Corinthians 13? There, love 'is not self-seeking' and 'does not delight in evil'. Clearly there is no relationship between the two. One 'love' destroys a marriage and brings untold misery to three children, while the other 'always protects, always trusts, always hopes, always perseveres'.

It is not possible to reject the authority of Scripture and still hold on to a moral code that takes the commands of God seriously. The world may call it old-fashioned and narrow-minded to believe the Bible, but the results of not believing are seen all around us in the breakdown of family life and the moral mess that characterises life at the beginning of the twenty-first century.

Tolerating sin
Evangelical Christians today tolerate what they would have strongly rejected twenty-five years ago. It is not that this toleration stems from a more generous spirit; it is, rather, the

result of not adhering, as they once did, to the teaching of Scripture. To tolerate what God denounces is a recipe for disaster. Examples of this toleration abound in our attitude towards the Lord's day; the breakdown of marriages of Christians; the number of evangelical ministers guilty of adultery; what we allow our children to watch on TV. The list is long and frightening.

It is true that years ago the behaviour pattern of evangelicals was dictated by tradition as well as Scripture. It may be that we were too narrow in some areas of our lives and these things needed dealing with, but today we seem to have thrown out the baby with the bathwater. If the boast of the Pharisee was that he was not like other men, it seems that today many evangelicals boast that they are exactly like other men. This inverted Pharisaism stems directly from an attitude to Scripture that is not worthy of a person who claims to love the Lord Jesus Christ.

The fact is that the Bible teaches that Christians are totally different from anyone else. Their standing before God is different—they are justified not condemned; their eternal destination is different—they are going to heaven not hell; and their lifestyle should be different. Paul writing to the Ephesians says, 'I . . . insist on it in the Lord, that you must no longer live as the Gentiles do' (Ephesians 4:17). Most of the rest of the letter following this verse tells us how the Lord expects his people to live. The detail of these instructions can leave no Christian uncertain as to what is expected of him or her. 'You were once darkness, but now you are light in the Lord. Live as children of light' (5:8). The apostle then goes on to say in verse 10 that the crucial thing for the believer is to 'find out what pleases the Lord'.

There is only one place to find out what pleases the Lord,

and that is in the Bible. If we do not believe the Bible we are left with our own inward desires. Our thinking will be moulded not by the will of God but by some godless newspaper editor or trendy TV producer. The only way to live like a Christian is to *think* like a Christian, and the only way to think like a Christian is to spend more time listening to what God is saying in his Word. This is why we should believe and live by the Bible.

Without the Bible we have nothing to say to the world that is any different from the moral, and in some cases immoral, platitudes that come from the lips of men who do not know God. We have no substitute for Scripture. An evangelicalism that proclaims the love of God but at the same time avoids the basic New Testament teaching on sin, guilt and judgement, and the need for repentance, is an evangelicalism that is sending souls to hell. It is impossible to be saved without repentance, and repentance is not possible without conviction of sin, and there will be no conviction unless men and women are confronted with their sin.

Why believe the Bible? Let A. W. Tozer have the last word:

Within the circles of evangelical Christianity itself there have arisen in the last few years dangerous and dismaying trends away from true Bible Christianity. A spirit has been introduced which is surely not the Spirit of Christ, methods employed which are wholly carnal, objectives adopted which have not one line of scripture to support them, a level of conduct accepted which is practically identical with that of the world—and yet scarcely one voice has been raised in opposition. And this in spite of the fact that the Bible-honouring followers of Christ lament among themselves the dangerous, wobbly course things are taking. So radically is the essential spirit and content of orthodox Christianity changing these days under the vigorous leadership of undiscerning religionists that, if the trend is not stopped, what is called Christianity will soon be something altogether other than the faith of our fathers. We'll have only Bible words left. Bible religion will have perished from wounds received in the house of her friends. The times call for a Spirit-baptised and articulate orthodoxy.

10
Using the Bible

Psalm 119 is the longest psalm in the Bible, and its structure is fascinating. There are 22 sections of 8 verses, each headed with a letter of the Hebrew alphabet. The most prominent characteristic of the psalm is a love for the Word of God. Most of the 176 verses refer to God's Word under different names—laws, statutes, ways, precepts, decrees, commands, word.

Verse 105 sums up the unique place Scripture has in the life of a Christian: 'Your word is a lamp to my feet and a light for my path.' We are living in a world that is morally and spiritually dark. There are no longer any absolute standards because moral attitudes now change from one generation to another. How, then, is the Christian to live? Are we to be governed by the world's changing and decaying standards or do we have an absolute, unchanging authority? Psalm 119 makes it clear that God's Word is a lamp that shines brightly and clearly for those who have eyes to see it.

What is the Word of God?
The Bible is a unique book. There is nothing quite like this remarkable collection of 66 books written over a period of 1,500 years by 40 authors. It is crucial that we appreciate the uniqueness of Scripture. If the Bible is only a collection of old myths, then it would be stupid to accord it any authority. But the Bible claims to be much more. Its message is essential for

salvation—'faith comes from hearing the message, and the message is heard through the word of God' (Romans 10:17). It is also essential for spiritual growth—'As newborn babes, desire the pure milk of the word, that you may grow thereby' (1 Peter 2:2 NKJV).

When we say that the Bible is the Word of God, we do not mean that God actually wrote it. He is its primary author, but it was written by human authors. But these were not expressing their own opinion—'Above all, you must understand that no prophecy of Scripture came about by the prophet's own interpretation. For prophecy never had its origin in the will of man, but men spoke from God as they were carried along by the Holy Spirit' (2 Peter 1:20-21).

These inspired authors were guided and directed by the Holy Spirit. This does not mean that God dictated everything to them word by word. Inspiration is not mechanical. Moses and Paul were not secretaries taking down dictation; they were men carried along by the Holy Spirit. God directed their thoughts so that they faithfully expressed his mind (1 Corinthians 2:13). So the Christian can trust his Bible and rely upon it. Jesus said the Scripture cannot be broken (John 10:35) and he confirmed this by the way he himself used Scripture. He used it to resist Satan (Matthew 4:11); to deal with a seeking soul (Matthew 19:16-22); to answer his enemies (Matthew 15:1-9); and to explain the meaning of the cross (John 3:14).

The purpose of the Bible is to reveal God to us. There are two types of revelation. There is the revelation of God in his creation, of which Psalm 19 speaks when it says, 'the heavens declare the glory of God; the skies proclaim the work of his hands' (v.11). This revelation is called 'general' because it is accessible to everybody (see Romans 1:18-20). But sin has so blinded man's heart that this revelation will never lead to salvation. So a special revelation was needed, not only to show us the beauty and order of creation, but to show also the ugliness and disorder of human nature dominated by sin and the remedy in God's grace in Jesus. This special revelation is the Bible.

How should we use the Bible?

We will never use the Bible effectively unless we love it. The Psalmist set the right example for us when he said, 'Oh, how I love your law!' (119:97). If we truly believe that the Bible is the Word of God, then we ought to love and treasure it. Love is more than admiration and respect. Why did William Tyndale give his life so that we could have the Scriptures in English? It was not because he admired this amazing book, but because he loved it.

Such a love will determine how we use the Bible. If like the Psalmist we can say, 'Oh, how I love your law!', then the next part of the verse will be inevitable—'I meditate on it all day long.'

Several years ago I went to preach at a church in Spain and took two young men from my church with me. One fell in love with a girl in the Spanish church. Their love for each other was obvious, but language was a problem. He could not speak Spanish and she could not speak English. As soon as we returned to England, this young man enrolled in evening classes to learn to speak Spanish. He had no interest in Spanish before, but now he loved this girl and desired to express his love in words she could understand. Love will always motivate action, and it will enable the action to be not a burden but a delight. If we love God's Word, then we will give time to meditate upon it—not occasionally when we feel like it, but day and night (Psalm 1:1-2).

The regular daily use of the Bible is crucial. If, as the apostle Peter says, the Bible is spiritual food for our soul and promotes spiritual growth, then daily feeding is obviously necessary. One of the major hindrances to spiritual growth is indwelling sin, and God's answer to this is Scripture—'I have hidden your word in my heart that I might not sin against you' (Psalm 119:11). Meditation implies thought, time and effort. It is quite the opposite to a casual dipping into Scripture. The person who is meditating is serious and not in a hurry. You will never benefit much from a reading of the Bible that is too quick and shallow.

No real Christian would deny the need for a daily use of Scripture, but very often the spirit is willing and the flesh is weak. How many times we make good resolutions to be more diligent in our Bible study, only to revert back to our old ways in a few weeks! So how do we combat this? Start by loving God's Word: if you do this you are halfway there. But you need also to recognise that there are two areas of Bible use—reading and studying.

Reading
This must be daily and systematic. Do not fall into the trap of reading in a haphazard way—dipping in here and there to your favourite passages. The result of that will be that you know a few passages well, but the bulk of Scripture will remain a mystery to you. To overcome this, most of us need a system of Bible reading. There are many such systems available—some that enable you to read through the whole Bible in a year. But don't be too ambitious. Choose a system you can cope with, or one that you can adapt to suit yourself. If you don't, you can easily fall behind the quota of readings and get discouraged and give up. Set a pace that you can handle, and stick to it. It

may be a chapter a day or ten chapters a day; only *you* know what your brain and workload can suitably benefit from. It is good also from time to time to read some of the shorter books of Scripture through in one sitting.

Ask your pastor or some older Christian what system of Bible reading they could recommend to you. System is crucial. If you fit in Bible reading when you can, then do not be surprised if you rarely fit it in at all. The devil will see to that.

What is the best time of day to read God's Word? There is no one answer to this, because it will vary with each one of us. Some people are useless in the morning, and others are useless late at night. A time when you can open the Bible with your mind alert and eager is the best time for you. The best time will differ also according to your responsibilities. A retired person with plenty of time is obviously different from a young mum with small children. Find out what suits you and stick to it. This involves self-discipline, but no one ever got anywhere in the Christian life without self-discipline.

Bible reading should always be linked to prayer. Each of these actually feeds and flows out of the other.

Bible study
This is different from Bible reading, and takes more time; therefore it may only be possible once or twice a week. For Bible study you need more than reading notes; you need a good commentary, a concordance, and perhaps a Bible atlas. Learn how to use these and make them regular tools. But ask your pastor before you buy—there's a lot of poor material on the market, and you don't want to waste your money.

Some Christians plead that they do not have time for Bible study. Once again the answer to this flows out of love for

God's Word. If you have time for your favourite TV programme you should have time to study Scripture. We would all have plenty of time for this crucial devotion if we used Sunday properly.

Using the Bible should be not an arduous task but a daily delight. When we know the Word it will really be like a lamp to our feet and a light to our path. Our spiritual life will be enriched, and that in turn will strengthen the spiritual life of our church.

11
Right and Wrong

There was a time when everyone knew what was right and wrong. Society had standards that were recognised, even if they were not always adhered to. Today all that has changed. Morality has died, and 'anything goes' has become the philosophy by which our nation lives or, perhaps more accurately, the philosophy by which it is dying. There is now no such thing as right and wrong, because there are no recognised absolute standards. So what was condemned thirty years ago, things like homosexuality, adultery, public nudity, foul language, are now acceptable. And to want to return to the old standards is regarded with total intolerance as puritanical.

Why has the change come about? Has there developed a more loving and gentle spirit in the land? No. The change is the result of a rejection of God and the Christian faith. It is not an expression of love, but an intolerance of anything that is biblical. For years we thought we could have the morality of the New Testament without the Christ of the New Testament. People would say that all we needed was the Sermon on the Mount and that Christian doctrine was divisive. Now even the Sermon on the Mount is regarded as too narrow and restrictive.

All this can be very confusing for a young believer. How can we live a Christian life in such a moral climate? We need to start by accepting that God's standards are absolute. For instance, what the Lord declared in the Ten Commandments thousands of years ago is still true today. It is still wrong to commit adultery or to covet. Moral standards are not to be dictated by the passing whims of society, but must be seen as the unchanging will of God. It may be that the world will never accept this, but the Christian must. Our standards must be those set out by God in the Bible, otherwise the Christian faith has no authoritative voice with which to speak to the world. A Christian faith which does not practise Christianity is a hypocrisy.

Conscience
Conscience is the God-given ability to distinguish between right and wrong. Paul argues that this is as true of the unbeliever as it is of the believer (Romans 2:15). Men and women are not animals, and they have more than instinct with which to react to situations. They have a mind and will, and conscience uses these. Conscience is to the mind what pain is to the body. It warns that something is wrong and needs to be dealt with. But the conscience is not infallible and needs a standard to refer to. 'Its role', says John MacArthur, 'is not to teach us moral and ethical ideals, but to hold us accountable to the highest standards of right and wrong we know.' The great problem of our nation at the beginning of the twenty-first century is that, having rejected God and the authority of the Bible, its standard of right and wrong is not very high. This is true not just of criminals but of society as a whole, and thus we tolerate moral filth in our homes via TV and videos that would have been utterly unacceptable thirty years ago. This inevitably blunts the conscience.

The conscience is meant to make us aware of personal guilt, but today we are urged to avoid feeling guilty. This often leads to society giving more sympathy to the criminal than to

68

the victim of crime. After mugging and brutally beating an old man in the subway in New York, Bernard McCummings was shot when running away from his crime. He was permanently paralysed and sued the New York Transit Authority for damages. He won $4.8 million. The man he mugged, a cancer patient, is still paying medical bills. McCummings, the mugger, whom the courts regarded as the greater victim, is now a multimillionaire.

By its abysmally low standard of right and wrong, and its refusal to accept guilt, society has effectively silenced the conscience. As a new Christian you are saved out of that kind of background and, in your new life, its influence has to be resisted and avoided.

A new standard
The Christian's standard has to be the unchanging Word of God. Submission to the authority of Scripture in our everyday lives is the means by which sanctification (growth in holiness) is worked in us. The purpose of sanctification is to make us like Christ. This is God's desire for us and it ought to be the chief ambition of every believer. It is not easy, and if our standards are not the same as Christ's it will be totally impossible. So we need to learn to think biblically, to absorb the teaching of the Bible so thoroughly that it permeates our thinking and governs our desires. In this way our conscience will have the highest possible standard to which to relate.

When the Bible becomes our standard we will start to take God seriously, and only then will it be possible to take sin seriously. This will enable us to recognise our weaknesses and deal with them. We will be unable to tolerate what God hates. The greatest danger in the Christian life is to accept our sins as inevitable. If we believe we can do nothing about our sin, our doctrine of sanctification will be hopelessly wrong, because we are told very clearly in Romans 6 that we are dead to sin and we are not to let it reign in our bodies. Sin is no longer our master; therefore it cannot compel us to do anything. Sin can only operate in the Christian with his or her co-operation.

Withdrawing that co-operation is what the Bible calls putting sin to death. This is an obligation for all believers (Romans 8:12-13).

Putting sin to death involves the application of our new biblical standards in our lives. This we do not merely by will power but by Holy Spirit power. It is the Holy Spirit who enables us to mortify sin or put it to death. John MacArthur says, 'The instrument of mortification is the Holy Spirit, and his power is the energy that works in us to carry out the process. All the means of mortification are simply commands of Scripture that we are called to obey.' MacArthur then goes on to list some of the key commands:

Abstain from fleshly lusts (sinful desires)	1 Peter 2:11
Make no provision for the sinful nature	Romans 13:14
Fix your heart on Christ	1 John 3:2-3
Meditate on God's Word	Psalm 119:11; Joshua 1:8
Pray without ceasing	Luke 22:40; Matthew 26:41
Watch and pray	Psalm 19:12-14
Exercise self-control	1 Corinthians 9:25-27
Be filled with the Holy Spirit	Ephesians 5:18

12
Doubts

Doubts are the seeds that the devil sows in the heart, mind and conscience of a Christian to rob him of the joy of salvation. No Christian is immune to this. In fact, if you never have any doubts at all, then your salvation would have to be seriously questioned.

> Intellectual believers are never troubled at all, they are always perfectly at ease, without a doubt or any trouble. They say, 'Ever since I made my decision I have never had a moment's trouble.' Such talk is always indicative of a very dangerous condition, is always very suspicious because it is too good to be true.
>
> *D. M. Lloyd-Jones*

As you read the biographies of some of the greatest men of God you find that some time or other they all had doubts. The young Charles Spurgeon had his share, but it did not prevent him becoming the greatest preacher of the nineteenth century.

> I remember times, in my earliest Christian days, when there came into my mind thoughts so evil that I clapped my hand to my mouth for fear I should be led to give utterance to them. This is one way in which Satan tortures those whom God has delivered out of his hand. Many of the choicest saints have been thus molested. Once, when I had been

grievously assailed by the tempter, I went to see my dear old grandfather. I told him about my terrible experience, and then I wound up by saying, 'Grandfather, I am sure I cannot be a child of God, or else I should never have such evil thoughts as these.' 'Nonsense, Charles', answered the good old man; 'it is just because you are a Christian that you are thus tempted. These blasphemies are no children of yours; they are the devil's brats, which he delights to lay at the door of a Christian. Don't you own them as yours, give them neither house-room nor heart-room.

C. H. Spurgeon

Doubt and sin

Doubts come very often when you have sinned in thought, word or deed. The devil then accuses, 'You cannot be a Christian, or you would never have thought like that or behaved like that.' And such is your sense of guilt and sorrow for the sin that you begin to believe him. Do not let him deceive you. Your sense of guilt and sorrow are proof that you are a child of God. Before conversion sin produced no such feelings in you. You are a Christian, so away with the doubts!

Sin in the Christian is always wrong and inexcusable; but, praise God, it is always pardonable. Read 1 John 1:7-10. These words are written to Christians. Nowhere does the Bible teach sinless perfection. When you sin, do not begin to doubt your salvation. Confess your sins, and remember 1 John 2:1. You have an Advocate, One who speaks to God for you.

Doubt and suffering

Doubts also come at times of sufferings and sorrow. You begin to feel sorry for yourself and you doubt whether God is with you. In such situations, heed the advice of John Elias:

I myself know much of fears, depressions, tossings within, but it was useless to make my complaint known to any one. It was well for me many a time to draw near to God; I know He delivered me for the sake of His great name, which ground only I had to plead before Him.

Read also Psalm 73.

Doubt and faith
Doubts are not good and no one wants them, but you must never think that because you have doubts you have no true faith.

> There may be true faith where there is much doubtings. Witness those frequent sayings of Christ to His disciples, 'Why are ye afraid, O ye of little faith?' (Matthew 6:30; 14:31; 16:8; Luke 12:28). Persons may be truly believing who nevertheless are sometimes doubting. In the same persons that the fore-mentioned Scriptures speak of, you may see their faith commended and their doubts condemned, which doth necessarily suppose a presence of both.
>
> *Thomas Brooks*

The way to deal with doubts is to remember their source. They come from the devil, so heed the advice of Spurgeon's grandfather: 'Don't you own them as yours, give them neither house-room nor heart-room.' Above all,

> When Satan tempts me to despair,
> And tells me of the guilt within,
> Upward I look, and see Him there
> Who made an end of all my sin.
> *Charitie Lees De Chenez*

13
Assurance

The greatest answer to doubts is a strong assurance of salvation.

> Such is Satan's envy and enmity against a Christian's joy and comfort, that he cannot but act to the utmost of his line to keep poor souls in doubt and darkness. Satan knows . . . that assurance is that which will make men strong to do exploits, to shake his tottering kingdom about his ears; and therefore he is very studious and industrious to keep souls off from assurance, as he was to cast Adam out of paradise.
>
> *Thomas Brooks*

This assurance is something that God wishes all his people to have (Hebrews 10:22).

Assurance is not presumption or arrogance, and it is certainly not intended to be the experience of only a few special Christians. Read the whole of Romans 8. It starts with 'no condemnation' (v.1) and ends with 'no separation' (v.39). No condemnation for whom? you ask—'for those who are in Christ Jesus'. This means all Christians, every Christian—great apostles like Paul and little nobodies like you and me. No separation for whom? It is Paul who is writing, and he says, 'I am persuaded' (v.38 AV) or 'I am convinced' that nothing can separate *us* from the love of God. Thank God for that word *us*. It includes all God's people.

So, you see, assurance is for us all. Without it you will be continually plagued with doubts. You will for ever live a weak, timid Christian life. You can be a Christian and not have this assurance, but to have it is to have your heart enlarged by the gospel. There is a joy and thrill about assurance which, amidst all the problems described in Romans 8:35-36, give purpose, direction and stability to the Christian life.

Assurance is the fruit that grows out of the root of faith.
Stephen Charnock
Assurance is glory in the bud, it is the suburbs of paradise.
Thomas Brooks
Faith is our seal; assurance of faith is God's seal.
Christopher Nesse

How does one get this assurance?
You can begin by looking at your own life in the light of Scripture, in order to see the difference salvation has made. You love righteousness now and hate sin. You love going to church now, whereas before it bored you. Prayer and the Bible have a new meaning for you. All these things give you grounds for assurance that you are a Christian. But you need more than this.

So now you look at the cross and see what God has done for you. Notice how Paul delights in this in Romans 8:31-34. When you see the greatness of God's love in Christ it empties you of all self and pride. When you gaze upon the cross you will always be made to feel your own sinfulness and the wonder of God's love. To realise that you now react to the cross in this way gives you further grounds for assurance. But it is still not enough.

It is when the Christian is aware of the depravity and

sinfulness of his own heart, and also aware of the amazing grace of God, that the Holy Spirit pours into his heart the great seal of assurance in which the apostle Paul delights in Romans 8:16.

Commenting on Romans 5:5 (AV), 'And hope maketh not ashamed, because the love of God is shed abroad in our hearts by the Holy Spirit which is given unto us', Dr Lloyd-Jones says:

This is the highest form of assurance possible to the Christian. It is a form of assurance, I repeat, that you do not deduce. There are forms and types of assurance that can be deduced. You can argue, Scripture tells us 'Whosoever believeth is not condemned.' I believe, and therefore I am not condemned, therefore I can be sure. That is quite right. You can go further and say, 'I go to the First Epistle of John and I read there the tests of life and of sonship. I examine myself in the light of these tests, and finding evidence of these things in me I deduce that I am a child of God.' That also is good; it is another form of assurance and a higher and better one than the first. But the highest form of assurance is the one we have here. You do not deduce the love of God here; the Holy Spirit sheds it abroad in your heart. The same thing is described in this Epistle in chapter 8:16, 'The Spirit itself [himself] beareth witness with our spirits that we are the children of God.'

Assurance of salvation does not rest primarily upon feelings and emotions. Its base lies in what the Scripture says God has done for you and is now doing in you. But it is an inferior assurance that does not know and feel and experience the love of God. You will never get assurance by trying to persuade yourself that you are saved. Ask God to give it to you. He will, for he has promised to do so (1 John 5:13).

Many new believers lose assurance by spending too much time looking at their failures. We need to be conscious of our weaknesses, otherwise we cannot deal with them; but a pre-occupation with these can be disastrous for assurance. Assurance of salvation depends upon justification, not sanctification. In other words, it depends upon what Christ has done for us, not what we are doing for him. We are saved by grace, not works, and it is grace that keeps us Christians. If our assurance depends upon how prayerful or obedient we are at any given point, it will be up and down like a spiritual yo-yo. But if it depends upon the grace of God in Christ, it will remain steady.

14
Failure

It is not unusual that after the early weeks of enthusiasm and excitement the new convert finds himself or herself going through a period of trials and doubts. During this time, sins you thought you had got rid of, once and for all, reappear in your life. You feel confused and bewildered, and failure seems to be stamped all over your new Christian life. Is this the end? Will God still love and trust you?

The answer is, it is not the end, and God never stops loving you. Face the fact that you have failed. Sin in the Christian is failure—failure to love, honour, serve and obey God. But God does not cast away failures. Failure will hinder your sanctification for a time, but it will not affect your justification. You are still saved. You are still a child of God (see chapter 2). The Scriptures are full of examples of Christians who failed miserably, but whom God went on to use mightily.

Take, for example, John Mark. Here was a young Christian who failed miserably. Read Acts 12:25–13:13. He left Paul and Barnabas at Perga, and Acts 15:36-41 makes it clear that he deserted them. The problems and trials of spreading the gospel were too much for him, and he ran away. Because of this Paul refused to take Mark on the next missionary journey.

Mark had failed. Yet years later Paul refers to Mark as his fellow worker in the gospel (Colossians 4:10-11), and even today we benefit from Mark's work for God as we read the second book in the New Testament. Here was the failure who

made good. Be encouraged by this. We have a loving and for-
giving God, who does not toss us upon the scrap heap of failure as quickly as we might do with one another. Did not Peter
fail (Mark 14:68)? Yet look in the book of Acts and see how
mightily he was used by the Lord afterwards.

Failure is not to be dismissed as unimportant. It is an awful
thing. It grieves God and causes problems for other Christians
(Acts 15:39). But it is not the end of our usefulness in the service of God. We must be particularly careful not to allow past
failure to be like a great weight hindering our present and
future progress (Philippians 3:13-14).

Learning from failure
Have you failed in some aspect of your Christian life? If so,
you must learn from that failure. Find out where you went
wrong, and determine not to do the same thing again. The
devil intends to use failure to dishearten you, but by the grace
of God you can use it as a springboard to victory. Let your
failure teach you your need of complete dependence upon
Jesus Christ (John 15:1-5).

In the Old Testament, Ebenezer was the place of Israel's
greatest failure, and also the place of a great victory. At
Ebenezer the people of God lost the Ark of the Covenant to
their enemies the Philistines (read 1 Samuel 4:1-22). Here was
terrible failure, and it was the direct result of neglecting the
things of God. Read now chapter 7 of 1 Samuel and see how
Ebenezer (v.12) became the place of victory. It was the same
God, the same place, the same people, the same enemy; yet
instead of defeat and failure there was victory. Why?

v.2   they lamented after the Lord—they wanted God,
           they cried to God with earnestness and urgency.

| vv.3-6 | they repented of the sin that had caused defeat and failure. |
| v.8 | they put their trust in the Lord, and in him alone. |

The result was that all that had been lost was restored (vv.13-14).
The next time you fail, remember Ebenezer!

> Here I raise my Ebenezer,
>   Hither by Thy help I'm come,
> And I hope by Thy good pleasure
>   Safely to arrive at home . . .
>
> Prone to wander, Lord, I feel it,
>   Prone to leave the God I love;
> Take my heart, O take and seal it,
>   Seal it from Thy courts above!
>   *Robert Robinson*

15
Backsliding

Backsliding is the most terrible and pathetic condition a Christian can get into. Most of us, at some time or other, and to some degree or other, are guilty of this. There are degrees of backsliding. There is the obvious backslider, who stops going to church and cuts himself off from all other Christians. Thank God, most of us never experience this. But there are times when our heart and our thinking become worldly. You may never stop going to church, the outward form of religion may still be maintained, but the heart has backslidden.

Backsliding does not necessarily mean that you get drunk every Saturday night. It means that your heart is not right with God. Like Demas, you have 'loved this world' (2 Timothy 4:10). The backslider is the Christian whose heart has gone astray. He has become weary of the things of God—the church, fellowship, prayer, the Bible—and his eye has wandered to the old 'pleasures of the world'. He begins to hanker after and to long for the things that God forbids. Long before his feet wander away, his eye and heart have backslidden.

The whole process is often a very subtle one. No one wakes up one morning and decides to backslide. You just stop praying for a couple of days, or maybe cut out the prayer meeting now and again. On a cold Sunday morning you stay in bed a bit longer and miss the morning service. It is only for this week, you assure yourself; you will be there next Sunday morning. This is the beginning of backsliding; it creeps upon you very gradually.

The result of backsliding is that the Christian becomes unfaithful, unreliable, and extremely critical of other believers. He will very often complain about lack of fellowship in the church, and yet at the same time resent the efforts of other believers to point him back to the Lord.

The greatness of God's love
Backsliding is a terrible condition to be in. It grieves God. The devil rejoices. But the backslider is still a Christian. He cannot lose his salvation (John 10:28-29); God still loves him. David, who had an awful experience of backsliding (Psalm 51), declares, 'he restores my soul' (Psalm 23:3). God never stops loving his people, and some of the most remarkable passages in Scripture are those in which we read of God yearning over his backslidden people. In these passages some of the most vivid descriptions of the love of God are to be found.

The two prophets who were used by God to express this aspect of his love were Jeremiah and Hosea. Read carefully and prayerfully Jeremiah 3:12-19. Then turn to the remarkable book of Hosea. God sent this prophet to marry the prostitute Gomer (1:2-3), in order that he might serve as an illustration of God's love for a prostitute people who had turned from God's love to idolatry (3:1). Read chapter 14:1-4. This is the greatness of divine love: even in our backslidings God loves us and will restore our souls.

God saves us by his sovereign power, but he does not use this power to prevent us from backsliding. The redeemed soul is a free soul. Before salvation there was only bondage (Ephesians 2:1-3); but redemption sets us free to enjoy and obey God. The Lord wants us to love him with a free heart, but if

82

we go away and backslide, he demonstrates again the depth of his love by his willingness to forgive and restore.

Restoration
Restoration is possible on the ground of repentance. The back-slider in his sin can feel sorry for himself. That is not repentance. Repentance means that you realise that even if you are not found out by others and no one else knows about it, God knows your sin, and you are grieved because you have sinned against this holy and loving Father. Repentance produces a prayer similar to David's in Psalm 51. God always hears this kind of prayer. Praise God, 'he restores my soul (Psalm 23:3).

There is only one place for a backslider to go, and that is, in a spirit of true repentance, back to his God, who will 'heal their waywardness and love them freely' (Hosea 14:4). He can restore in a moment 'the years the locusts have eaten' (Joel 2:25). The long months or years of backsliding that have hardened the believer's heart can be wiped away in a moment, and the joy of salvation restored. There is no probationary period; it is done at once.

If you have found your spirit beginning to backslide, go at once in prayer to God. Ask him to show you where you first began to go wrong. Confess your sin to him, and ask for forgiveness. He will forgive and restore.

16
Guidance

How can I know God's will? What does God want me to do? These are familiar questions to all Christians, for the matter of guidance can be a real problem.

Some Christians, in seeking to grapple with this question and make guidance simple, have devised various methods for discovering God's will. One of these methods, which we can only describe as the 'lucky dip', is for the Bible to be opened at random and the finger haphazardly pointed at a verse. This verse, then, irrespective of its context, becomes 'God's will' for the particular situation. Avoid this method like the plague! The story is told of a man who tried it, and the first verse he pointed at was Matthew 27:5—'Judas . . . went and hanged himself.' Finding that this did not help, he tried again, only to come up with Luke 10:37—'Go, and do thou likewise.' How true the story is I do not know, but it does serve to illustrate the absurdity of such a method. There *are* times, of course, when God speaks to us very strongly through a verse of Scripture. At such times he brings the verse to our attention and rivets it upon our mind. This is quite different from what we mean by the 'lucky dip'.

Some Christians rely very much upon subjective or 'inner' feelings, and they say rather glibly, 'The Lord has told me . . .' God does reveal his will in this way, but one should always check such alleged guidance with what the Holy Spirit has revealed clearly in the Bible. The Spirit of truth will never lead a person to do anything which he has already forbidden in Scripture.

Guiding principles

The Psalmist said, 'Your word is a lamp to my feet, and a light to my path' (Psalm 119:105). This reminds us that in the vast majority of the situations we have to face in everyday life, the Scriptures give us clear guidelines as to what is God's will. If the Bible forbids something, you do not need any further guidance on that matter—you must obey. If the Bible says that you must do certain things, again it is obedience that you need, not guidance. If you follow faithfully day by day the guidelines laid down clearly in the Scriptures, you will find when you come to the major and more difficult decisions of life that God will reveal his will clearly to you. Daily submission to the will of God in the ordinary routine of life will make it much easier to discern God's will in the bigger things.

Although subjective feelings can be dangerous, they cannot be dismissed altogether, because the Holy Spirit acts *upon* our spirit, and not separately from it. A strong feeling or conviction about a matter could be the work of the Holy Spirit; or, again, it could be the product of our own carnal desires. How are we to distinguish between the two? Ask yourself the following questions. Have I prayed about this matter? Have I earnestly sought to find out what the Scriptures have to say? Am I willing to do whatever God wishes? If these things are true of you, then you have reason to believe that the Holy Spirit is leading you.

Sometimes guidance can be a problem because we do not really want to know God's will. We have decided beforehand what we intend to do, and are merely looking for some kind of assent to ease our conscience. If you find yourself asking three or four Christians for advice on a certain problem and they all tell you the same thing, and yet you still go on asking others, the probability is that you are not interested in knowing God's will, but you are merely looking for someone to agree with what you have already decided to do.

Yet another difficulty arises from the fact that when God has clearly revealed his will, we can misunderstand it because of personal feelings. This was the case with Agabus, Luke and other believers in Acts 21:10-14. Their love for Paul and their concern not to see him imprisoned coloured their thinking. Our motives can be the highest, and yet our judgements may be wrong. We must all come to the position where we say 'The will of the Lord be done'—no matter what the cost.

The problem of guidance is really the problem of communion with God. The great men of the Scriptures rarely seemed to have much trouble in this realm. They lived close to God, and because of this his will was clear to them. That is why Christians should *never* make major decisions when they are in a low condition spiritually. In such a condition they are unlikely to know God's will and will almost certainly make the wrong decision.

When in doubt
In the more difficult decisions of our lives—as, for example, where we ought to worship, where we should live and work, and other major issues which fortunately arise only rarely—the following advice from John Flavel is helpful:

If therefore, in doubtful cases, you would discover God's will, govern yourself in your search after it by these rules:

• Get the true fear of God upon your hearts; be really afraid of offending him.

- Study the Word more, and the concerns and interests of the world less.
- Reduce what you know into practice, and you shall know what is your duty to practise.
- Pray for illumination and direction in the way that you should go.
- And this being done, follow Providence as far as it agrees with the Word, and no further.

David's statement in Psalm 23 is also most helpful: 'He guides me in paths of righteousness.' God always leads in a path that will produce godliness and righteousness in us. So if the decisions you are likely to take will mean that you have less time for prayer, Bible study and fellowship, it is almost certain that God is not guiding you that way. God guides us always towards himself, never away from himself.

If God's guidance is not clear to you in any given situation, whatever you do, do not take things into your own hands. If God is closing doors before you, do not in frustration and impatience try to push one open. God will open the right door at the right time. He always does (Acts 16:6-10). Do not rush. Trust God, and he will make his will known to you.

One last word. Do not try to be over-spiritual about guidance. Most issues are solved by a simple but prayerful application of scriptural teaching and common sense.

17
Self-discipline

For most of us there was very little self-discipline or order about our lives before we became Christians. We did things either because we had to do them (for example, going to school or to work), or because we liked doing them (for example, sport or music). In most areas of our lives self-discipline played very little part. But once a person becomes a Christian, that has to change. Over and over again the Bible exhorts us to discipline ourselves. We constantly read phrases like 'make every effort' (2 Peter 1:5), 'purposed in his heart' (Daniel 1:8 AV), 'press towards the goal' (Philippians 3:14), 'put off . . . put on' (Ephesians 4:22-25), and all these phrases speak of self-discipline.

Its importance
You may feel that self-discipline does not sound very spiritual; all that matters, surely, is that we should have faith. Faith, of course, is crucial; but you need to realise that without a disciplined life you will stagnate as a Christian.

I defy you to read the life of any saint that has ever adorned the life of the church without seeing at once that the greatest characteristic in the life of that saint was discipline and order. Invariably it is the universal characteristic of all the outstanding men and women of God. Read about Henry Martyn, David Brainerd, Jonathan Edwards, the brothers

Wesley, and Whitefield—read their journals. It does not matter what branch of the church they belonged to, they have all disciplined their lives and have insisted upon the need for this; and obviously it is something that is thoroughly scriptural and absolutely essential.

D. M. Lloyd-Jones

Have you noticed that whereas you can read a newspaper or a novel for a considerable time without any trouble, after five or ten minutes of reading the Bible you feel tired and put it down? The same is true of prayer. You can watch a television programme for an hour or more without losing concentration, but after a very short time in prayer your mind begins to wander. Why is this? It is the work of the devil.

There is a kind of general indolence or laziness which afflicts us all and is undoubtedly produced by the devil himself. Have we not all noticed that when it comes to things in the spiritual life, we do not seem to have the same zeal and enthusiasm, nor do we apply the same energy as we do with our secular calling or vocation, our profession or business, our pleasure, or something we happen to be interested in?

D. M. Lloyd-Jones

There is only one way to deal with this. You must 'resist the devil' (James 4:7). Notice that in order to do this you must first 'submit yourselves . . . to God'. The problem will not go away of its own accord.

James [in his epistle] has no recipe for instant sanctification. He knows no easy way to victory for the Christian.

From the start he warned us that we are still in the world (1:1), subject to endless pressures (1:2), and by resisting them we were walking the God-appointed pathway to maturity (1:3,4). Here is the battle, and here is the path. He will not allow us to evade the conflict and cast away the crown. Victory is not ours for the taking, but ours for the winning.

J. A. Motyer

Self-discipline means that irrespective of your feelings you do what is right. It means also that you refrain from doing what is wrong, even though there may be a strong desire and a natural tendency to do it. Read Ephesians 4:17-32.

Its benefits
There is no aspect of our spiritual life that will not benefit greatly by daily self-discipline. For Bible study and prayer it is essential. Setting a time and sticking to it is not being legalistic; it is a right and proper approach to the things of God. How easy it is to waste a great deal of time on trivialities, and then to plead that we have no time to feed our souls!

Discipline does not take all the joy, spontaneity and excitement out of the Christian life. On the contrary, because it deepens our relationship with God, it adds to our joy, spontaneity and sense of expectancy. Can you think of a more disciplined man than the apostle Paul—and was there ever a man more filled with the Holy Spirit and the joy of the Lord?

So many people say that they would give anything to have but a vestige of the knowledge that the saints had. 'If only I had that joy, I would give the whole world for that—why cannot I have the experience of the warm heart?' they say.

The answer is that they have never really sought it. Look at the lives of those men and the time they gave to Scripture reading and prayer and various other forms of self-examination and spiritual exercises. They believed in the culture and the discipline of the spiritual life and it was because they did so that God rewarded them by giving them these gracious manifestations of Himself and these mighty experiences which warmed their hearts.

D. M. Lloyd-Jones

No army knows victory if it is undisciplined, and no Christian will know victory without strong and determined self-discipline.

18
Work

The next three subjects that we shall deal with—work, marriage and the sabbath—are called 'Creation Ordinances'*, because they were given to man by God at the beginning of his life here on earth. Read Genesis, chapters 1 and 2.

It does not matter whether you are a teacher or a pupil, an employer or an employee—everyone has to work. God made this very clear in Genesis 2:15. Adam was not meant to live a life of pleasant idleness in the Garden of Eden; he was to 'dress it' (that is, to till or work it). This was before sin entered man's nature. Work was something intended or ordained for man from his creation.

The Christian view
The Christian view of work is taught clearly in Ephesians 6:5-9. We are to do as we are told (v.5a) and do it with proper respect ('fear and trembling' AV) and with unmixed motives (v.5b). We are not to be guilty of 'eyeservice', that is, working only when we are being watched. It follows therefore that all able-bodied people should work when work is available—even though some may think it 'pays' to be on social security.

This view of work is completely different from the attitude commonly found today. Note verse 7 particularly: 'Serve wholeheartedly, as if you were serving the Lord, not men.' If you

*see Acknowledgements, p.132

cannot do your job like this, then you should ask yourself if you are in the right job—that is, the job God wants you to do.

The right job is the one you are physically and intellectually capable of doing, and, more importantly, the one you can do with all your heart and perform as God requires you. It is the job in which you can use your God-given abilities to their full capacity. It will also be a job that will not cause you to undermine biblical principles and that will not weaken your spiritual life. We would all like to have highly paid, interesting jobs, but it is far more important to be in the place where the Lord wants you. Honest work is not degrading. It may be boring, hard or even unpleasant, but doing it 'as if you were serving the Lord' will transform your attitude to it. A man who empties dustbins conscientiously is helping to keep a town free from disease, and his work is as vital as that of the most highly qualified doctor.

The right attitude
The Christian may not be the most skilful worker, but he ought to be the most conscientious. A Christian in school may not be the brightest in his class, but he ought to be the most hard-working. His work should be in on time and should always be done to the best of his ability. Whether he likes a particular teacher or not, he should be polite and reliable.

We spend more time in working than in any other activity. Therefore our attitude to our work is of crucial importance if we are to show non-Christians the difference Christ makes to our life. Slackness and carelessness are characteristics that should never be seen in a Christian. He or she should always be an example of conscientiousness, reliability and punctuality. In addition to Ephesians 6:5-8, read Titus 2:9-10 and 1 Peter 2:18-20. These Scriptures are not suggestions that may be heeded or discarded at your convenience. Substitute for 'slave' the word 'employee', and you see what God requires of you in your working life. You are employed not to evangelise but to work, and if you fail to follow these Scriptures any evangelism in your place of employment will be hollow and futile. Unless your Christianity makes you a better worker in the factory, office or school, it will have profited you very little. And until you faithfully discharge your God-given responsibilities in work, it is unlikely that God will ever call you to any ministry in the church.

There is a difference between wanting to get on in your job in order to use your God-given talents to their fullest capacity, and groping your way up the promotion ladder in order to bolster your pride and your income. Many Christians have got themselves into serious spiritual difficulties on account of moving their jobs—and consequently their home and church—just because the new job was better paid. There is nothing wrong in being promoted and having a bigger salary, but do not let that be your only yardstick. Seek God's leading.

If moving your job means moving church, be particularly careful. Make sure that you will still be able to attend a church where you will be taught God's Word and can have fellowship with other believers.

19
The Lord's Day

There is only one reference in the Bible to 'the Lord's day' (Revelation 1:10), but there are a great many references to 'the sabbath'.

As to the expression 'the Lord's day', this is one of the titles of the sabbath. It intimates that the change of day from the seventh to the first of the week is by Christ's authority, for 'Lord' always brings in the thought of authority. 'The Son of man is Lord also of the sabbath' (Mark 2:28) was a strong hint that He was about to change the day. It is equally correct for us to term Sunday 'the Lord's day' or 'the sabbath'.

A. W. Pink

The question that concerns many young Christians (and older ones too) is, How are we to regard Sunday? Do all the Old Testament instructions still apply? To answer this question, first read the Ten Commandments (Exodus 20:1-17). Note carefully the fourth commandment (vv.8-11).

It is significant to note that this is the only one of the Ten which opens with the word 'Remember', as though men had the greatest tendency to forget it! That word 'Remember' also plainly intimates that this Sabbath commandment was not given at Sinai for the first time, for the

Israelites of Moses' time could not 'remember' something which they had never heard of before! I mention this because erroneous teachers are fond of declaring today that the 'sabbath' is entirely Jewish, that it began and ended with the Mosaic dispensation. This is a serious mistake.

A. W. Pink

In other words, the sabbath did not begin with Moses and the Ten Commandments, but is one of the 'Creation Ordinances' given to man at the beginning of time in Genesis chapters 1 and 2. These three ordinances, work, marriage and the sabbath, were meant by God for the good of all men for all time.

Some people quote Mark 2:27—'The Sabbath was made for man, not man for the Sabbath'—as proof that Jesus abolished the old restrictions. This is not so. Jesus vigorously opposed the Pharisees' view of the sabbath with their list of dos and don'ts (mainly don'ts). He restored the balance between the worship of God (which he upheld by his own regular example) and the good of men—'The Sabbath was made for man'.

The New Testament makes it quite clear that from the resurrection of Christ onwards the Christians met for worship on the first day of the week rather than on the seventh day. In view of the glorious events of the first Easter they evidently felt able to change the day, but they were not at liberty to change the basic pattern of one day in seven, as this was laid down in the creation ordinances.

What should the Christian do on Sunday?
We must not fall into the trap of the Pharisees and make a list of dos and don'ts. Neither must we be so loose in our attitude

that we break the fourth commandment. In Exodus 20:8-11 there are two basic truths.

First, we are to *keep the day holy*. This means that we are to use our sabbath to worship God. We worship him every day, but on Sunday we come together to worship God, not as individuals but as a church, and we are able to give more time to worship. On Sunday we especially give thanks to God for our salvation through the death and resurrection of Christ. It is a day of triumph—an idea superbly expressed by Isaac Watts in his hymn, 'This is the day the Lord hath made'.

> Today He rose and left the dead,
>   And Satan's empire fell;
> Today the saints His triumph spread
>   And all His wonders tell.

So, if there are two church services on a Sunday, we ought not to be satisfied with attending only one of them! Many Christians complain that they have no time for Bible study and reading Christian books. If they used Sunday properly they would have plenty of time.

Secondly, it is a day when we *cease from work*. The word 'sabbath' means 'rest'. God, having created us, knows that we need one day's rest in seven. Many people try to be wiser than their Creator and ignore this provision he has made, but they often pay for it in later life. There are certain jobs which have to be done on a Sunday (Luke 13:11-16). Doctors, nurses and others have to work, and certain family duties have to be done. Digging the garden, cleaning the car, school homework, etc., do *not* come into this category.

For notwithstanding this rest and cessation from labour

which is required on the Lord's day, yet three sorts of works may and ought to be performed . . . these are works of piety, works of necessity, and works of charity.

Ezekiel Hopkins

What fitter day to ascend to heaven, than that on which He arose from earth, and fully triumphed over death and hell? Use your Sabbaths as steps to glory, till you have passed them all, and are there arrived. *Richard Baxter*

Sunday is the LORD's day. We are to use it to glorify our God and Saviour. Sunday observance is based upon the great principles of worship, rest and love. Do you love God? Then remember his day and keep it holy.

20
Marriage

Marriage is not just a social custom which has evolved over the years and can be cast aside by society as out of date. Marriage is ordained by God. It is something that goes back to creation (Genesis 2:18,21-25). Our Lord's teaching on marriage (Matthew 19:3-9) and that of the apostle Paul (Ephesians 5:21-33) both refer to this creation passage.

One of the main purposes of marriage is companionship throughout life. 'It is not good for the man to be alone', said God (Genesis 2:18). It involves a union closer than any other on earth ('bone of my bones . . . one flesh'), a union that will continue while bodily life lasts (vv.23-24), It is a closer bond than that of blood relationships—'Therefore shall a man leave his father and his mother' (AV). Our Lord referred to this statement in Genesis in order to show how serious it is for anyone to break up a marriage (Matthew 19:3-6), and as presenting the reason why partners must remain ever faithful to each other (v.9).

This does not mean that God intends all his people to marry. Some do not feel the need for marriage; others are deprived of it by circumstances, and a few may deliberately forgo marriage in order to serve God. But usually most Christians will marry. What do you think of the following statement?

No man ought seriously to contemplate matrimony until

(1) He is in a financial position properly to support a wife—otherwise he is 'tempting' the Lord and presuming on His providence. (2) Till he has, in some goodly measure, learned by grace to rule his own spirit (Proverbs 25:28), otherwise he will be a plague to his partner and not a 'help-meet'! (3) Until he is sure that God has brought him into contact with a truly regenerate girl, who is likely to be congenial, equally yoked, and a help to him. In seeking a wife neither good looks nor money should influence him. Moral qualities and spiritual graces last when physical beauty has faded and money taken to itself wings.

A. W. Pink

It is of crucial importance that a Christian should marry another Christian (2 Corinthians 6:14). Do not fall prey to the idea that if you are a Christian and your partner is not, you will be able to win him/her over. It rarely works out like that. More often than not, the Christian becomes lukewarm towards Christ or, with one partner pulling one way and the other pulling the opposite way, he/she has a tremendous struggle throughout married life to survive.

Marriage is a union—two persons becoming one. Partnership is too weak a word to describe it. It is a union so blessed and a oneness so complete that Paul does not hesitate to compare it with our Lord's union with his church. Read carefully Ephesians 5:21-33. All young Christian couples, before marriage, should study this passage together. Dr D. M. Lloyd-Jones's exposition of the passage—*Life in the Spirit, in Marriage, Home and Work*—is particularly recommended.

Christian marriages, like every other kind of marriage, have their problems. Sometimes one hears older couples boasting that they have been married for fifty years or more without ever having had a cross word with their partner. Well, in rare cases that may be true, but it may well be that they have short memories! Tensions and disputes will come, but the old saying is still true—'Couples who pray together, stay together.' If you pray together daily, tensions cannot last too long.

We have already seen that Christians ought not to marry unbelievers. But often a Christian is converted *after* marriage, and so the situation is created where one partner is a Christian and the other not. Paul deals with this in 1 Corinthians 7:12-16.

If you find yourself in this kind of situation you must be very careful. Your greatest desire will be to see your loved one saved. But do not start preaching to your partner. Very often this will only aggravate the position. You must, of course, explain clearly what has happened to you, but you must remember that your partner is still in darkness and cannot understand. At first he/she may resent your new life which seems to exclude him/her. Be patient, take it slowly, pray much. What will win your loved one is not your words but your life. Let him/her see more kindness, more love, more understanding. You should now be a better husband/wife than ever you were before. Be careful not to rush around to meetings and neglect your home.

It may be months or years before your loved one is saved, but do not give up hope. Pray much for grace that you may keep your witness in the home sweet and yet firm.

21
Relationships

For young men and women to feel attracted to each other and to start dating is both natural and normal, yet for the Christian it can be a period fraught with very real dangers.

Some teenagers are very attractive physically and as personalities. They have no trouble at all in attracting boy/girl friends. In many cases this 'popularity' is quite harmless. For some young people, however, it can be a problem because, to put it bluntly, it feeds their ego. And when, for a Christian, self and pride become the centre of everything, there is very real danger of a spiritual landslide. Furthermore, when a teenage Christian's life is dominated by this sort of relationship it can spoil fellowship with other Christians, and ultimately it will inevitably spoil one's fellowship with God.

This is one of the prime ways the devil has of disrupting and breaking up a young people's group in a church. One becomes jealous of another, and there develops a tendency to vie for someone else's boy/girl friend. Obviously this is fatal to fellowship. Eventually, as often happens in teenage relationships, the couple will break up. This causes tension, and not a little pain, and for some it has even meant that they stop attending church.

All this is obviously very wrong, and it is the direct result of immature Christians indulging in a relationship which is too intense. Boys and girls have always been attracted to each other, and our purpose here is not to say that this is wrong, but to point out the dangers and to give some guidelines. For the Christian every situation in life has to be assessed in terms of how it will affect my relationship with God and my fellowship with other believers.

Some guidelines

- Your boy/girl friend must be a Christian. This was mentioned in the chapter on marriage, but it cannot be repeated too often. The Old Testament is full of warnings about this (Exodus 34:14-16; 1 Kings 11:1-4). The New Testament also states it very clearly: 'Do not be yoked together with unbelievers. For what do righteousness and wickedness have in common?' (2 Corinthians 6:14). There can be no exception to this rule.
- Your boy/girl friend must be a Christian, but this does not mean that any Christian will do. This may seem a rather obvious thing to say, but it is amazing how many young believers have started a relationship with boy/girl friends who are completely unsuited to them. Their temperaments, their interests and everything else about them seem to clash, and once again the result is pain and tears.
- What if your Christian boy/girl friend attends another church? In this case do not be too quick to start sharing services—his church one Sunday and yours another. Your first loyalty is to your own church, and that is where you ought to be on Sundays. That does not mean that you do not visit each other's churches occasionally, but you should not do so regularly, for then you will belong nowhere, and you will fail to contribute to the life of any church as fully as you ought. If your relationship blossoms into engagement, and marriage is soon to take place, that is the time for you

to consider prayerfully where to worship together. It will be essential when you are married that you worship together in the same church.

- In your early or mid teens relationships should never be too intense. If they are, someone is going to get hurt. When you reach your late teens and early twenties things are different, and it is important then that you are not too casual in your relationship. What might be merely platonic to you could well be intensely serious to your boy/girl friend. In such situations you can easily cause deep hurt to your friend.

In time friendship will become love. You are two young Christians who love each other. You believe that the Lord has brought you together, and you believe it to be his will that you should marry and spend the rest of your lives together. The months before marriage can be very difficult, because we live in an age when sex before marriage is regarded as normal and is indeed positively encouraged. Because you love each other you will want to consummate that love in sexual union. But sex before marriage is wrong. It is wrong, not because sex is dirty and sinful, but because it is beautiful and God-given. God intends it to be the ultimate expression of love within the bond of marriage. God's pattern is spelled out in Genesis 2:24, and this is enforced by our Lord, who quotes these words in Matthew 19:5, and by the apostle Paul, who repeats them in Ephesians 5:31. To 'leave his father and mother and be united to his wife' is an expression which refers to marriage, and only after that do the man and woman become 'one flesh'. 'Whatever else this may mean', comments William Hendriksen, 'as to oneness in mind, heart, purpose, etc., basically as the very words (*cleave, flesh*) in their combination imply, the reference is to sexual union, compare 1 Corinthians 6:16.'

Unbelievers will laugh at all this as being old-fashioned. But this is the Word of God, and as a Christian you must live by it. So you must never allow yourselves to get into a situation where your feelings run away with you. Love can be shown in a variety of ways before marriage, but you must never allow your sexual desires to control you. If you do, you will regret it later.

The months before marriage should be a time when you frankly and earnestly share your views on a whole host of things. It should be a time when you forge the basis of a deep spiritual fellowship. It is then that you learn to pray together and encourage and help one another to go on with the Lord.

How should couples view the time of their engagement? Should they not use it to explore each other's hearts and minds rather than each other's bodies? How clearly have they discussed their marriage goals? How explicit have they been in expressing what each expects of the other in marriage, in duties and interests shared or divided, finances, Christian behaviour in the home, the training of children? These are not issues decided by ticking off squares on a computer card. How easily can the couple talk about their deepest emotions? Their likes and dislikes?

John White

22
Parents and
Home Life

Unfortunately many teenage Christians in the early years after conversion have problems with their parents.* This arises primarily from a reluctance to accept the parents' authority and from a failure to understand what the Scriptures teach concerning family life. The Bible has a great deal to say about the attitude of children to their parents.

Read the fifth commandment in Exodus 22:12. To 'honour' someone is to hold them in esteem, to show them a spirit of respect and consideration, to have a high regard for them. 'Honour' is love plus respect and obedience. Notice that it is more than love; there is an element of duty and responsibility implicit in this commandment.

In Leviticus 19:3 (AV) the Lord God commands everyone to fear his mother and father. The word 'fear' means to revere, to hold in deep affection, or to respect. Note that mother is placed first with regard to respect, whereas father is mentioned first in the commandment of Exodus 20:12. As a member of the weaker sex, mum often receives more abuse and dishonour from her offspring than father does. Young people will answer her back far more readily than they would their father. The command to honour and obey applies to both; respect is shown by a gentle, polite and responsive spirit.

*see Acknowledgements, p.132

106

The Christian will also show respect for his parents by being careful of the way he speaks about them to others. Parents are not our equals; they are our superiors under God. Their faults and weaknesses should not be related to others. When their weaknesses and failings are evident to those outside the family, the Christian child will try to offer the best explanation possible in order to excuse their behaviour: 'love covers over a multitude of sins' (1 Peter 4:8).

In the Old Testament the laws concerning the child's behaviour towards his parents are very strict. See, for example, Deuteronomy 27:16, where the term 'dishonour' means 'to consider of little account'. When you turn to the New Testament the example of our Saviour is clear. Living for thirty years in an ordinary home with Joseph and Mary and his brothers and sisters, our Lord knew the pleasures and problems of family life. Although Lord of glory, he was subject to his earthly parents (Luke 2:51). Even when in dreadful pain upon the cross, he was still deeply concerned about his mother's well-being. From the cross he made arrangements for his beloved disciple John to take care of her. John took her to his own home and treated her like his own mother (John 19:26-27). In the New Testament epistles too you will find the apostle Paul equally insistent that we are to obey our parents (Ephesians 6:1-3).

What the apostle tells the children is that they should obey their parents. This obedience, moreover, should flow not only from the feeling of love, gratitude and esteem for their parents, though these motivations are very important, but also and especially from reverence for the Lord Jesus Christ. Paul says that it should be an obedience in the Lord, and he adds, for this obedience is right. The proper attitude

107

of the child in obeying his parents must therefore be this: I must obey my parents because the Lord bids me to do so.

William Hendriksen

A testing ground

The greatest testing ground for any professing Christian is his own home. Whether our parents are believers or unbelievers, it is in the home that the stresses and strains of life bring to light the true nature of our hearts. Just think back for a moment over the past twenty-four hours and recall some of the encounters (if not clashes) which have taken place within your own family. Tensions arise in the best families—indeed, the devil seems to muster his strongest attack on this front. On the other hand, as the differences of opinion and clashes of personality that are part and parcel of intimate family life test the reality of our Christian experience, there can be no better place to show the fruit of the Spirit (Galatians 5:22-23).

If you have born-again, believing parents, do you realise what a privilege this is? It is not unusual to hear teenage Christians complaining about their Christian parents, and nearly always the complaint centres upon their authority. They will not let you go to a disco, watch certain programmes on TV, stay out late, etc. Your friends at school seem to be enjoying these things, and you feel hard done by, and complain that your parents are being old-fashioned and narrow-minded.

Your parents act like this because they love you. They see you as a gift from God and they know that God has given them a responsibility for your total well-being—body, mind and spirit. This responsibility they take very seriously, and rightly so. They know from experience (which you do not have) that certain things will harm you. It is because they love you that they prevent you from doing things non-Christian parents see no harm in.

If your parents are not Christians and do not share your love and enthusiasm for the Lord, this will inevitably cause some difficulties for you. They may not be willing for you to go to church as often as you would like. You must be very careful not to react in such a situation with insolence and cheek. The fifth commandment is still applicable: you must honour your father and mother. It is no Christian answer for you to do things behind your parents' back, even though all you are doing is attending church. What you must do is to let your new life in Christ prove to them that God is real to you and in you. In practical terms this means being more helpful around the house, being less selfish and more considerate. Let your Christianity show in the home, not with pious words that Mum and Dad cannot understand, but with loving, caring actions that speak volumes.

Such situations can be extremely difficult, but stubborn rebellion is no answer. You are a Christian, so act like one. Prayer and patience must be exercised. Later on, when you reach the age of eighteen or thereabouts, even though the fifth commandment still applies, you can graciously and kindly thank your parents for their advice and concern, but quietly insist that you are going to follow Christ.

23
Money

Years ago there was a popular song which ran 'Money is the root of all evil'. Like so many popular things in the world, the song was wrong. The Bible says, 'For the *love* of money is a root of all kinds of evil' (1 Timothy 6:10). Money is neither good nor bad in itself. It is man's attitude to it that causes trouble.

What should be the Christian's attitude to money? Read 1 Timothy 6:7-19. We should certainly not love money. Neither should we regard money as evil. Without it the church could not maintain its ministry and its missionary work. The Bible teaches us that we are stewards of all God has given us, including our money. Whether we have a lot or a little, it is to be used wisely for the glory of God. It needs to be stressed that whether we are rich or poor, we are stewards of what we have, and the Bible's teaching on the use of money governs the conditions of poverty and of wealth.

How should we use our money? It is to be used to provide the necessities of life for ourselves and for our family (housing, clothing, food, etc.). This is a duty laid upon us in the Word of God (1 Timothy 5:8). Money is to be used also for pleasure and recreation (books, holidays, etc.). It is God's will that we enjoy this beautiful world which he has made, but the Christian must be careful not to waste his money on the passing fancies of the world.

The Bible makes it clear, however, that the Christian is a

person who gives money away, and who does so not now and again grudgingly, but regularly and cheerfully (1 Corinthians 16:1-3; 2 Corinthians 9:7). This giving is done generally in three directions: (a) to our local church; (b) to a missionary work; (c) to a charity. Very often money given to the local church covers these three aspects of giving, as the church both uses and distributes the money received. Another way of giving, which is a beautiful expression of Christian love, is what the Authorised Version of the Bible calls 'almsgiving' (Luke 12:33; Acts 9:36; 10:2). This is when you see an individual or a family in need, and without any fuss (Matthew 6:1-4) you help with a gift. All giving produces a sense of joy in the giver (Acts 20:35), but almsgiving is particularly satisfying.

Tithing
The question that bothers many is, How much should I give? The basis of the Old Testament teaching was tithing. Read Leviticus 27:30-33; Deuteronomy 12:6-18; 14:22-29; 2 Chronicles 31:5; Nehemiah 10:37. Basically this meant that one-tenth of a person's income was given to the Lord. In the New Testament, tithing is nowhere commanded as a requirement for the Christian. There is a great emphasis upon *giving*, but not on tithing. However, this does not mean that tithing has no bearing upon the Christian's life. If, before Christ came, God's people gave one-tenth of their income to the Lord, should it be any less for those of us who have known the full revelation of the love of God in Jesus Christ? Clearly it should be more.

All your money is God's. The practice of giving one-tenth of our income is a good one in order to secure that necessary channelling of our money into the work of God, but we do not understand things aright until we acknowledge that all our possessions are His in the very first place.

E. F. Kevan

One-tenth is a good place to start giving to the Lord. But our giving is not to be legalistic, but spiritual. We give not because we must, but because we love and are loved. We are to give out of the prosperity the Lord has given us (1 Corinthians 16:2). Notice how the apostle Paul, when he is dealing with the question of giving money to others, introduces two remarkable descriptions of God's great gift to us: 'For you know the grace of our Lord Jesus Christ, that though he was rich, yet for your sakes he became poor, so that you through his poverty might become rich' (2 Corinthians 8:9); and 'Thanks be to God for his indescribable gift!' (2 Corinthians 9:15).

This is the way we are to give, with our hearts filled with the knowledge of God's love to us, and of how much we owe him. Our giving is a response to God's giving: 'Freely you have received, freely give' (Matthew 10:8).

> Were the whole realm of nature mine,
>   That were an offering far too small;
> Love so amazing, so divine,
>   Demands my soul, my life, my all.
>
> *Isaac Watts*

You can only give your money to God as an act of worship in this way if you have first given yourself (2 Corinthians 8:5).

Give prayerful thought to the following words of J. C. Ryle:

I entreat all professing Christians to encourage themselves in habits of liberality towards all causes of charity and mercy. Remember that you are God's stewards, and give money liberally, freely, and without grudging, whenever you have an opportunity. You cannot keep your money for ever. You must give account one day of the manner in which it has been expended. Oh, lay it out with an eye to eternity while you can!

I am thoroughly persuaded that the income of every religious and charitable Society in England might easily be multiplied tenfold, if English Christians would give in proportion to their means.

I believe that in giving to support works of charity and mercy, we are doing that which is according to Christ's mind—and I ask readers to begin the habit of giving, if they never began it before; and to go on with it increasingly, if they have begun.

24
Abortion

Abortion is probably the greatest social evil in Britain today, and no Christian can be immune to its effects in one way or another. Abortion is the deliberate and, as far as society is concerned, the legal destruction of millions of babies since the 1967 Abortion Act. It is currently running at about 170,000 a year or 500 abortions every day. If this had happened in Old Testament times, could you imagine Isaiah or Amos or any prophet being silent? Isaiah chapter 59 describes society 700 hundred years before Christ was born, and it is a description that frighteningly fits our society today:

For your hands are stained with blood, your fingers with guilt . . . No-one calls for justice; no-one pleads his case with integrity. They rely on empty arguments and speak lies; they conceive trouble and give birth to evil . . . Their feet rush into sin; they are swift to shed innocent blood . . . So justice is driven back, and righteousness stands at a distance; truth has stumbled in the streets, honesty cannot enter. Truth is nowhere to be found, and whoever shuns evil becomes a prey. The LORD looked and was displeased that there was no justice (vv.3,4,7a,14-15).

Abortion is a reflection of man's attitude to God and the God-given gift of life. It has become so accepted in Britain and the USA that one child out of every three or four conceived is deliberately put to death in the womb. The statistics are horrifying. Every year in the USA, three times more babies are killed than the total number of American soldiers killed in the Second World War! The womb has become more deadly than the battlefield. John Stott writes,

> We need to revise our vocabulary. The popular expressions help us to conceal the truth from ourselves. How can we speak of 'termination of a pregnancy' when what we really mean is the destruction of a human life? We need to have the courage to use accurate language. Abortion is feticide, the destruction of an unborn child.

The present situation

The 1967 Abortion Act decreed that if two doctors acting in good faith decide that an abortion is advisable for any of four stated reasons, then it is legal. The wording is so inept that almost any pregnancy could be legally aborted, and in reality 170,000 abortions occur every year.

Our concern is not with cases where abortion is necessary to save a mother's life. Thankfully this is a rarity. Of the 177,225 abortions performed on women in England and Wales in 1996, only 138 involved risk to the life of the mother, and in only 1,943 cases was there a risk that the child would be born handicapped. The general situation virtually amounts to abortion on demand. The deciding factor is the so-called right of the woman to kill the baby because 'It's my body, and I can do what I like with my body.' One argument often put forward is that it is not a baby, only a foetus; therefore all the talk of killing babies is emotional nonsense. But the facts are that 21 days after conception, even before most women are sure they are pregnant, the baby's heart is beating; and after

- 1 month—baby has head, eyes, nose, mouth and a brain.
- 6 weeks—brain patterns can be measured.
- 2 months—baby will grab an instrument placed in its hand.
- 9 weeks—baby can suck its thumb.
- 3 months—baby can kick its legs and feet, has its own fingerprints and starts to breathe through the umbilical cord.

It is already fully formed, and by the time it is born the baby has been living for 9 months. An abortion takes away that life, and our society accepts this as normal. We quite rightly recoil in horror when a terrorist bomb kills a few people, but we don't bat an eye at the fact that 170,000 babies are killed every year. We are in an absurd situation: our courts have actually awarded compensation to unborn children involved in a car accident; yet they take no action about the practice of the deliberate killing of unborn children. Unborn babies have been operated upon; a 16-week-old foetus in the womb has had a life-saving operation to prevent kidney failure. And yet we still kill such creatures of God! John Stott writes,

> The key issue, then, is a moral and theological one. It concerns the nature of the foetus (foetus is Latin for offspring). How are we to think of the embryo in the mother's womb? For it is our evaluation of the foetus that will largely determine our attitude to abortion . . . We reject as totally false and utterly abhorrent the notion that the foetus is merely a lump of jelly or blob of tissue, or a growth in the mother's womb, which may therefore be extracted and destroyed like teeth, tumours or tonsils.

What does the Bible say?
Human life is a precious gift from God. The first chapter of the Bible makes that clear. The fact that man is made in the

116

image of God is basic to our whole approach to life in general, and especially to the evil of abortion. But when does life begin? The Bible is clear that life begins not at birth but at conception. Ruth 4:13 tells us that conception is a gift from God. Listen to the beauty of Psalm 139:13-16.

> For you created my inmost being; you knit me together in my mother's womb. I praise you because I am fearfully and wonderfully made; your works are wonderful, I know that full well. My frame was not hidden from you when I was made in the secret place. When I was woven together in the depths of the earth, your eyes saw my unformed body. All the days ordained for me were written in your book before one of them came to be.

We are told in Exodus 21:22-25 to respect the pregnant woman and the child she carries.

The unborn are always treated in Scripture as human—they can move and leap (Luke 1:41), can be consecrated for God's use (Jeremiah 1:5, Galatians 1:15), can be filled with the Holy Spirit (Luke 1:15). All these verses make it clear that there is life in the womb, and to take away that life is to destroy a human being.

What should Christians do?

In Britain the 1967 Abortion Act needs repealing, but that is not likely as no government, even if it had the conviction, would have the courage to do it. We should not be too disheartened by this, as political action alone is not enough. Martin Luther King was right when he said, 'Morality cannot be legislated, but behaviour can be regulated. Judicial decrees may not change hearts, but they can restrict the heartless.' But even if we cannot change the law at the moment, we should still use our right as citizens to protest against this great social evil, and on a personal level seek to convince people of the wrong of abortion. Neither of these will be done unless we really care. Nothing we protest about or object to will have any credibility unless we care for the pregnant woman and the handicapped child. More information on how to do this can be obtained from Evangelicals for LIFE (Life House, Newbold Terrace, Leamington Spa, CV32 4EA).

It's tough being a Christian in today's world. Standing up for Christ and for Christian standards at work, in the community, and in the nation, demands courage and integrity. Secular values are constantly being pushed by the media, in education and in the social and caring services. But man cannot ignore God's moral laws and get away with it. The Bible says, 'A man reaps what he sows' (Galatians 6:7). Actions have consequences, and all around us in Britain today we see the consequences of ignoring biblical teaching on the family, on law and order, and with respect to medical and sexual ethics.

It is the Christian faith which works in practice. Even though policy-makers may not accept the Bible as God's Word, Christians can still point to the consequences of rejecting God's laws. Even research by secular social scientists shows that the permissive revolution of the 1960s has profoundly damaged the health and well-being of children and adults. Whether the issues are clear-cut or complex, there is a desperate 'need to speak out for what is right. We must spell out the moral implications of legislation and public policy' (The Christian Institute).

25
Drugs

Not drugs again! It's all we seem to hear about these days, at school, in the newspapers, and on television programmes! Why is there all this emphasis on drugs?

We need not look further than a recent United Nations report to see how seriously we are challenged by drug abuse.

> No nation, however remote a corner of the globe it occupies, however robust its democracy, is immune to the adverse consequences of drug abuse, and countries whose social fabric is weak are particularly vulnerable . . . Drugs are taken for the relief of pain, for the treatment of disease, to change mood, to find or lose identity, to forget and to explore. The body and sometimes the mind can so crave these sensations that their absence becomes intolerable and drives some users to extremes . . . Science has not yet taught us to predict who will become a slave and who a master.
>
> *World Drug Report*, UN World Control Programme

What is the truth about drugs? Are they a gift from God who 'richly provides us with everything for our enjoyment' (1 Timothy 6:17), or are they the result of man's ability to invent new evils?

We must recognise that many of the discoveries and advances of our present scientific age are mixed blessings.

Although they offer great benefits to mankind they also have the potential for misuse. This is true of many of the drugs we know today. Where appropriately prescribed, drugs can alleviate pain in seriously ill patients, but at the same time they have brought anguish and misery to many people.

The Bible and drugs

When we turn to our Bible dictionary we will not find the word 'drug', let alone the names of the modern 'designer drugs' with which we are so familiar. However, on the same page of our Bible dictionary we will find reference to the effects of a drug that was well-known in Bible times—drunkenness. There are many references to drunkenness and alcohol in the Scriptures and it is not difficult to find some positive things stated about wine. The psalm writer spoke about 'wine that gladdens the heart of man' (Psalm 104:15). However, we need to be very careful here, because many are references to 'new' wine connected with the harvest, and in our terms this would be not much different from our fruit juice. An example of this is found in Nehemiah (10:39).

The Bible gives a clear picture of the consequences of drinking alcohol. Drunkenness is always condemned. Wine is described as 'a mocker and beer a brawler' (Proverbs 20:1). Alcohol clouds sound judgement, and those in positions of authority, kings and princes, are advised to abstain. They need clear heads to dispense justice and apply the law without partiality (Proverbs 31:4-5). The same is true of those who lead the church (1Timothy 3:3). The book of Proverbs is full of advice on the use of this particular drug. Look up Proverbs 4:17; 20:1; 21:17; 23:21.

The harmful results of alcohol are seen all around us. It is the cause of much of the violence we see in families, on the streets of our towns and at football matches. Alcohol always produces a personality change and invariably this change is for the worse. It has always been the same. This can be seen in the story of Noah (Genesis 9:20-26). It can mean having to live with shame and sorrow. Consider the following passage from the book of Proverbs:

Who has woe? Who has sorrow? Who has strife? Who has complaints? Who has needless bruises? Who has blood-shot eyes? Those who linger over wine, who go to sample bowls of mixed wine. Do not gaze at wine when it is red, when it sparkles in the cup, when it goes down smoothly! In the end it bites like a snake and poisons like a viper. Your eyes will see strange sights and your mind imagine confusing things. You will be like one sleeping on the high seas, lying on top of the rigging. 'They hit me,' you will say, 'but I'm not hurt! They beat me, but I don't feel it! When will I wake up so I can find another drink?' (Proverbs 23:29-35).

How familiar is this picture! Nothing has changed in the two thousand and more years since these words were written. The effects of alcohol on behaviour and morals certainly haven't changed.

Christian viewpoint
As we have said, there is no mention of modern leisure drugs in the Bible, but much of what is true about alcohol is true of these also. A simple definition of a 'drug' is a substance that alters the way our bodies work. Most of the illegal drugs are mood-changing drugs. They alter the way the brain functions. Consider the Christian response to the following:

- If something makes a person talk more, does it also make a person think less? As you talk more, are you less or more careful about what you say?
- If something makes you more daring and less careful, (apart from driving) what do you put at risk?
- If your personality is slowed down or speeded up, what does that do to your temper? How does it affect your patience or your ability to serve, and to be alert and energetic to do good?
- If something is addictive and reduces you to slavery and dependency, can it be good?
- If something alters the balance of your life, so that it makes greater demands on your time and your money, reduces your self-control and your ability to think, is it advisable?
- If something puts at risk your health and how you get on with your family and friends, is it to be valued?
- If something could risk your life, and lead to prosecution or an act that leaves you open to ridicule and shame, how should you respond to it?
- If something feeds money into the criminal fraternity, which does not care about a person's health and safety, or the quality of life within our communities, is it a good thing for a Christian to do?

The threat of drugs will not go away. As we have said, drugs properly used and medically dispensed can be of great benefit, but in a day when drug-taking for 'kicks' is acceptable, the Christian needs to be able to give sound biblical reasons for his or her refusal to be involved in the drugs culture.

Life to the full
Life is to be enjoyed and we should live life to the full. This

is what Jesus said he had come to provide for his followers. Drug addiction is a thief (John 10:10). We should always aim to be the best we can for God who has given his best for us, not even sparing his own Son (Romans 8:32).

If life is to be full we need variety. We need physical exercise, good food, plenty of sleep, fulfilling relationships and life to present a challenge. There is no greater challenge than living a Christian life in an ungodly society, but what are the principles that govern Christian living?

- If we love God, we should look after our bodies which are temples of the Holy Spirit (1 Corinthians 3:16).
- We should produce fruit in our lives. The fruit of the Spirit is not like the fruit of drug-taking because it not only includes 'love and peace', but also 'gentleness and self-control' (Galatians 5:22-23).
- We should not always insist on the right to act as we see best. We have a duty to other Christians and those who are seeking the truth. It is easy to be obstacles to others (1 Corinthians 8:13).
- We should always be available as good Samaritans to help, restore and serve others.

Elsewhere in this book you will read of three young men who resisted pressure to conform to the world around them (Chapter 26, Peer Pressure). Many Christian young people of your generation are doing the same and refusing to be involved in the use of unnecessary and harmful drugs. God honoured the stand taken by Shadrach, Meshach and Abednego and promises to honour those who honour him. Jesus is still saying, 'Take up your cross and follow me.' This is sufficiently challenging and exciting for anyone.

Better than wine

We come to the end of a chapter on drugs without mentioning speed, whizz, dope and smack or any other designer drug that is in vogue when you read this book. We can be certain that the fashions of this world will always change, but the principles of Scripture remain the same. God always has something better than the things offered by the world. He says, 'Do not get drunk on wine . . . be filled with the Spirit' (Ephesians 5:18). If you want a buzz out of life let it be knowing and serving the Lord Jesus Christ. Why? The love of Jesus is 'better than wine' (Song of Solomon 1:2 NKJV).

The alcoholic longs for his next drink; the addict craves his next 'fix'; the Christian says he wants more and more of the love of Jesus. Don't let anything lessen that desire for more of Christ. So develop a spiritual hunger for God by filling your mind with the things that both create and satisfy such a hunger.

Finally, brothers, whatever is true, whatever is noble, whatever is right, whatever is pure, whatever is lovely, whatever is admirable—if anything is excellent or praiseworthy—think about such things. Whatever you have learned or received or heard from me, or seen in me—put it into practice. And the God of peace will be with you (Philippians 4:8-9).

26
Peer Pressure

Peer pressure is a striking feature of life today. Youngsters experience it at school when they are branded by their classmates as swots and discouraged from working hard at their studies. People at work come up against it when they try to blow the whistle on colleagues who are stealing materials from their employers. Managers who try to be fair to employees feel it when they are expected to ignore safety regulations in order to make greater profits.

Christians must certainly expect to face group pressure, especially at school, college or university. *For real Christians are bound to stand out from the crowd.* They have different values and different aims in life. They don't believe in getting drunk at the weekend. Nor are they into drugs. Nor do they go in for sleeping around, because they know that their bodies are temples of the Holy Spirit (1 Corinthians 5:19) which are to be kept pure from sexual immorality.

Because Christians are recognisably different (or should be!), they must expect to attract attention from their peer group. So, at university, they will be under pressure to join in drinking parties or to indulge in casual sex 'like everybody else'. Or, at their place of work, they may be mocked if they don't join in the telling of filthy stories.

How can a Christian resist peer pressure and stand firm out of loyalty to Jesus? First of all, a Christian must make a choice. *It is impossible to be in with the group and faithful to him*. It is one or the other, simply because our Lord's life and his way contradict what the group stands for. Jesus makes this crystal clear. 'If the world hates you, keep in mind that it hated me first. If you belonged to the world, it would love you as its own. As it is, you do not belong to the world, but I have chosen you out of the world. That is why the world hates you' (John 15:18-19). Could anything be plainer? A Christian has a stark choice to make. He or she can live Christ's way or the world's way, but not both at one and the same time.

Secondly, a Christian resists peer pressure by *maintaining communion with God day by day*. He keeps in touch with God by reading and meditating on God's Word, the Bible, and by *praying in* what the Holy Spirit is teaching him as he does so. Scripture exposes how false the values of this world are and shows us what are the values of a godly life (see, for example, 1 Timothy 6:6-10). If the world is not to squeeze us into its mould through peer pressure, we must have our *minds* renewed day by day through communion with God.

Thirdly, a Christian resists peer pressure by *keeping close company with another group, God's people, the church*. In this group a Christian finds support, guidance, encouragement. He or she is strengthened through prayer and enriched by the warmth of the fellowship. There is understanding and acceptance and help in living the Christian life. Ungodly talk, for example, finds no place in this group (Ephesians 4:29), but only talk which builds up.

Finally, a Christian can take heart from those who in the past have resisted pressure to deny their allegiance to God. Three young men stood firm even when they were threatened with death if they refused to worship the image of gold set up on the orders of king Nebuchadnezzar. They politely said: 'If we are thrown into the blazing furnace, the God we serve is able to save us from it, and he will rescue us from your hand, O king. But even if he does not, we want you to know, O king, that we will not serve your gods or worship the image of gold you have set up' (Daniel 3:17-18). Shadrach, Meshach and Abednego stood firm. So, with God's help, can you.

27
Further Reading

There is a vast selection of good Christian books published today which can be of great help to you. There are also a number of books that are not very helpful, so be careful. Before you buy a book, ask the advice of your pastor or some experienced Christian.

It is a matter of concern that Christians today do not read enough, and that the only books they do read seem to be rather sensational biographies. The following list of recommended books has been prepared as helpful reading in the first few years after conversion. Some of them are easy to read: others are more demanding. Whatever you do, do not give up on the harder books. If you only read 'easy' books, you will never grow in the Christian faith.

First, here are some books to help you to understand more about salvation and the Christian life:

Right with God by John Blanchard
Learning and Living by John Blanchard
Add to Your Faith by Sinclair B. Ferguson
What You Need to Know about Salvation by Peter Jeffery

The Bible is the inspired Word of God. You need to believe this in spite of the many attacks that are made on the Scriptures today. A book on this subject which could be called 'essential reading', though not so easy as the others, is:

Nothing but the Truth by Brian H. Edwards

If you are still at school, the question of evolution will be a very real problem. There are many good books available to help you, and the following are especially recommended:

Myths and Miracles by David C. C. Watson
Bone of Contention by Sylvia Baker

As a Christian you should know something of the history of the church. Such history is not boring—the thrilling account of God's dealings with his people is anything but boring! Easy-to-read introductions would be:

The Story of the Church by A. M. Renwick and A. M. Harman
Sketches from Church History by S. M. Houghton

There are a great number of biographies available. The following have been selected because they will encourage you in the Christian life and at the same time teach many vital truths:

Joni by Joni Eareckson. A Christian's trials, sufferings and triumphs.
God Made Them Great by John Tallach. Brief biographies introducing you to some outstanding Christians.
God's Outlaw by Brian H. Edwards. The story of William Tyndale who gave us the Bible in English.
The Young Spurgeon by Peter Jeffery. The early life of one of the greatest preachers England has ever known.

Doctrine is a word that many Christians seem to be afraid of. It simply means what we are taught and what we believe. Rather than shunning doctrine, therefore, we ought to give it top priority. Many books on doctrine can be rather 'heavy',

but here are some which are not too difficult if you are prepared to put some effort into your reading:

Knowing God by J. I. Packer
God's Words by J. I. Packer
Great God of Wonders by Peter Jeffery
God's Riches: A Work-book on the Doctrines of Grace by
    John Benton and John Peet
The Christian Life by Sinclair Ferguson
Bite-size Theology by Peter Jeffery

Growth in your experience of God is of vital importance,
and any of the following books by Sinclair Ferguson would be
of great help to you:

Grow in Grace
Discovering God's Will
Children of the Living God

A new Chrisitian needs to learn to appreciate the Bible, and
two books that would greatly help in this are:

How to Enjoy Your Bible by John Blanchard
Handle with Care by Sinclair Ferguson

Start your study of the Bible in the New Testament, and to
help you appreciate each book of the New Testament read

Stepping Stones by Peter Jeffery

which is a New Testament guide for beginners.

Going on with God and walking 'worthy of the Lord'
depends, among other things, on your daily reading and study
of the Bible. Most Christians find that daily reading notes can

be a great help. A good place to start is in Mark's Gospel, using the notes by John Blanchard entitled *Read, Mark, Learn.*

There are many daily Bible reading notes available and one of the best is Geneva Bible Notes, obtainable from Grace Publications Trust, The Christian Bookshop, Sevenoaks Road, Pratts Bottom, Orpington BR6 7SQ.

Other useful aids for Bible study are:

Searching the Word: A Method for the Personal Study of the Scriptures (Bryntirion Press).

M'Cheyne's Calendar for Daily Readings—a reading plan covering the whole Bible in one year (Banner of Truth).

Reading the Bible by Geoffrey Thomas. A booklet with much helpful advice and a daily reading plan covering the Bible in a year (Banner of Truth).

Firm Foundations by Peter Jeffery and Owen Milton. A two-month Bible reading course introducing the reader to some great chapters of the Bible (Bryntirion Press).

It is a good idea to build up a small collection of reference books to aid your Bible study. The following would help you for many years:

The New Bible Dictionary (Inter-Varsity Press)

A good Bible concordance

The Lion Handbook to the Bible (Lion Publishing)

Christian Handbook by Peter Jeffery is a straightforward guide to the Bible, church history and Christian doctrine. It provides in one handy volume a wide range of information which would otherwise only be found in much larger and more expensive volumes.

Acknowledgements

- For many of the points made in chapters 15,16 and 17 I am indebted to three lessons on 'Creation Ordinances' written by John Manton and published in *Go Teach Young Teens*.

- The contents of chapter 19 ('Parents and Home Life') are largely drawn from a lesson on this subject written by Gareth Crossley and published in *Go Teach Young Teens*.

- I am indebted to the Revd Eirian Rees for the contents of chapter 25 ('Drugs').

- I am indebted to the Revd David Kingdon for the contents of chapter 26 ('Peer Pressure').

Quotations are taken from the following publications:

L. Berkhof, *Systematic Theology* (Banner of Truth); Thomas Brooks, *Heaven on Earth* (Banner of Truth); E. F. Kevan, *What the Scriptures Teach* and *Now that I am a Christian* (Evangelical Press); H. R. Jones, *The Doctrine of Scripture Today* (Evangelical Press); D. M. Lloyd-Jones, Commentaries on Romans and *God's Way of Reconciliation—Ephesians 2* (Banner of Truth); Leon Morris, *The Cross in the New Testament* (Paternoster Press); J. A. Motyer, *The Tests of Faith* (Inter-Varsity Press); John Murray, *Redemption Accomplished and Applied* (Banner of Truth); C. H. Spurgeon, *Metropolitan Tabernacle Pulpit* (Banner of Truth) and *Morning and Evening* (Marshall, Morgan & Scott); A. W. Tozer, *Worship— the Missing Jewel of the Christian Church* (Christian Publications Inc.) and *Paths to Power* (Marshall, Morgan & Scott).

Other books by Peter Jeffery from Bryntirion Press

All Things New
—a simple, straightforward explanation of basic aspects of the Christian life for someone who has recently come to faith.

I Will Never Become a Christian
—addresses the arguments and excuses of the convinced unbeliever.

Seeking God
—a clear explanation of the gospel, written for the earnest seeker after faith.

Firm Foundations
—a two-month Bible reading course introducing readers to 62 key chapters of the Bible and to some of the most important teachings of the Word of God.

Stand Firm
—a young Christian's guide to the armour of God.

Christian Handbook
—a straightforward guide to the Bible, church history and Christian doctrine.

Our Present Sufferings
—why do Christians experience sickness and suffering? Biblical principles and practical outworkings explained and illustrated.

Following the Shepherd
—through the twenty-third Psalm. Written to exalt the Good Shepherd and to warm the heart of the sheep.

These are available from your local Christian bookshop or, in case of difficulty, from the publishers (postage extra):
Bryntirion Press
Bryntirion, Bridgend CF31 4DX, Wales, UK.

Beginning at the Beginning by Graham Harrison. 151pp. ISBN 1 85049 154 2

To get to grips with the Bible's story-line you need to begin at the beginning with the book of Genesis, for this, the first book of the Bible, provides us with the master plot which is developed in the rest of Scripture.

Genesis shows us why humanity is as it is—fallen, self-centred, trying to order life without God. It also tells us why our world is so full of conflict and suffering. And, even more important, it begins to prepare us for the amazing story of the action God has taken to bring us back to himself and to restore us to his image.

In eight chapters on the key themes of Genesis 1–12 Graham Harrison convincingly demonstrates how the first book of the Bible is the foundation for all that follows, up to and including the last—the book of the Revelation.

God Spoke to them—Character studies of Old Testament people by Peter Williams. 223pp. ISBN 1 85049 139 9

The Old Testament has many memorable characters. Some are notable examples of faith in God. The lives of others warn us against following in their steps. So in this book we meet people as different as Cain, who murdered his brother; Daniel, a young man who wouldn't be brainwashed; Hannah, a godly mother; and Caleb, a man of conviction and courage.

From their stories—and those of others—Peter Williams skilfully draws out spiritual lessons for today.

Encounters with God—Some lesser known characters of the New Testament by Peter Williams. 140pp. ISBN 1 85049 121 6

In twenty-four readable chapters Peter Williams draws out challenging lessons from stories of characters as different as Festus, the sophisticated pagan; Lydia, the first European convert; and Silas, the man who lived in the shadow of the apostle Paul. These and many others come alive as real flesh-and-blood people, so very like us in the temptations they knew, the struggles they experienced, and the pressures they faced from living in a pagan society.

Most of the characters are testimonies to the grace of God at work in human weakness, but a few are salutary warnings of the dangers of trifling with the gospel or making shipwreck of the faith.

Read with an open Bible and a prayerful spirit, this book will challenge you to a closer walk with God and spur you to share your faith with others.

True Happiness by D. Martyn Lloyd-Jones. 96pp. ISBN 1 85049 138 0

Everywhere people seek happiness, only to be disappointed in their search. This is because they seek it as an end in itself, whereas, Dr Martyn Lloyd-Jones maintains, it is only to be found in knowing God.

In this exposition of Psalm One, originally preached as four New Year sermons at the beginning of 1963, Dr Lloyd-Jones shows the profound difference between true happiness and all false substitutes that people try to put in its place.

Living Water by John Benton. 39pp. ISBN 1 85049 145 3

Many people today have an unsatisfied thirst for spiritual satisfaction. Revolting against the idea that materialism is an adequate basis for living (and dying!) they instinctively feel that there is more to life than simply meeting bodily needs.

Taking this sense of unsatisfied spiritual need as his starting point, John Benton shows how it can be met by Jesus Christ, who calls to all humanity: 'If a man is thirsty, let him come to me and drink' (John 7:37). In a vivid and compelling way Dr Benton opens up the meaning of Jesus' words and brings home to us the great truth that Jesus has new life to give to anyone who is really thirsting to experience it.